# P.S. FORGIVE YOURSELF FIRST

### 21-Day Journey To Embrace Healing, Release Regret, And Rediscover Your Worth

Blending Our Love, Maryland

Copyright © 2023 by Tuniscia Okeke

*Cover Design*:

Published 2023

Library of Congress Cataloging-in-Publication Data

ISBN: 978-1-962748-16-2 (Print)

ISBN: 978-1-962748-17-9 (eBook)

Printed in the United States of America

# P.S. FORGIVE YOURSELF FIRST

## 21-Day Journey To Embrace Healing, Release Regret, And Rediscover Your Worth

### TUNISCIA OKEKE

BLENDING OUR LOVE, INC.

# DEDICATION

I Am The Gift.

# Table of Content

Paying It Forward ........................................................ 1

Foreword ..................................................................... 5

Introduction ................................................................ 7

What It Is vs. What It Is Not ..................................... 11

Signs of Unforgiveness .............................................. 17

Practicing Self-Forgiveness ...................................... 27

PART 1: FORGIVENESS .......................................... 37

Day 1: Acknowledge Your Pain & How It's
Holding You Back ...................................................... 39

Day 2: Declutter Emotions Forgive The Offense.
Learn The Lesson. Release It ..................................... 47

Day 3: Explore/Find Source of Pain ......................... 53

Day 4: Identify Triggers ............................................ 61

Day 5: Unforgiveness Only Impacts You ................... 67

Day 6: I Didn't Deserve It .......................................... 73

Day 7: Receive the Gift of Self-Forgiveness ............. 79

PART II: HEAL ........................................................... 85

Day 8: Release The Mental Torment ......................... 87

Day 9: Dig Up Pain .................................................... 93

Day 10: Apologies Don't Heal Pain ........................... 99

Day 11: Your Emotions Matter ............................... 105

Day 12: Healing Takes Time Shield Out Drama ............... 111

Day 13: Resentment Equals Clinging ....................... 117

Day 14: Realistic Expectations ........................... 123

PART III: GROW ........................................... 129

Day 15: Commit to the Journey ............................ 131

Day 16: Plant & Water Healing ............................ 139

Day 17: Give Grace ....................................... 145

Day 18: Create New Habits ................................ 151

Day 19: Memories (Re-Write Your Story) ................... 159

Day 20: Set Boundaries ................................... 169

Day 21: Be Clear On Your Intentions ...................... 175

P.S. ..................................................... 181

# Paying It Forward

I'm sharing this message as the author of this 21-day journal on forgiveness, not just with words on these pages but with a story that has shaped my life's purpose. As I embark on this journey with you, I want to share the deeply personal and transformative experiences that led me to write, edit, and self-publish 35 books on forgiveness in less than a year.

My forgiveness journey began when I was 24, a pivotal age when life often feels like an open book, brimming with hope and dreams. Then, my mother called me on a seemingly ordinary Monday morning, and with those words, she unraveled the narrative of my life. She revealed that the man I had believed to be my father for all those years was, in fact, not my biological father.

The weight of that revelation was crushing. It was as if the ground beneath me had shifted, leaving me unsteady and disoriented. But what shook me to my core was not the revelation itself but the sudden rupture of trust in my mother—the person I had always looked up to as a paragon of love, trustworthiness, and honesty.

In the wake of this revelation, I spiraled into a deep pit of resentment, anger, and pain. I grappled with a profound sense of betrayal and felt adrift in a sea of unanswered questions. It was a turbulent period in my life, and for 17 long years, I carried the heavy burden of unforgiveness.

Then, something remarkable happened that would alter the course of my life forever. I noticed a pattern in my relationship with my children. They treated me with a lack of respect and love, leaving me bewildered and hurt. In desperation, I turned to prayer one day, seeking answers from a higher source.

God's voice whispered into my heart in that sacred space of prayer and introspection, revealing a profound truth: "I taught them how to love me by the way I loved my mother."

Those words struck me like lightning, piercing through the fog of my confusion. It was an awakening—a profound realization that, in my quest for revenge against my mother, I had unwittingly passed on the energy of resentment to my children. I had normalized my hurtful behaviors as the way we should treat our mothers.

On my 40th birthday, I consciously confronted my soul's deepest and darkest corners. I embarked on a journey of healing, self-forgiveness, and forgiveness of my mother. My primary motivation was to restore my relationship with my children and teach them how to pass on healing, love, and forgiveness to their children.

That six-year odyssey of healing was transformative beyond measure. It led me to write 35 journals, each addressing a facet of forgiveness and healing I encountered on my journey. These journals became my way of reaching out to others grappling with their forgiveness journeys.

Today, I extend a heartfelt invitation to you to embark on this 21-day journey with me. Just as my healing journey began with a single journal, this journal can be your compass for forgiveness, healing, and growth.

I send you loving energy as you navigate through the complexities of your forgiveness journey, and I hope these pages serve as a guiding light toward wholeness and inner peace.

With love and compassion,

Tuniscia O

# FOREWORD

## Message From God To Me (Tuniscia O)

## January 24, 2022

## THE DAUGHTER OF A KING

God speaking, "If you are the daughter of a King, then how should you behave? How do you walk into rooms? What conversations do you have? What are your expectations in life? What do you want when everything you could imagine is already provided? What would you ask for when you know it's ready and waiting for you?

Who would you call when you know they are ready and excited to serve the King's daughter? What conversations would you have when seeing the world's eagerness to help you? How would you love others when given everything?

What would your response be to those in need when you are in power? What would you say? What would you do, or how would you help those who hurt or betrayed you the most?

My daughter, you are the child of the most high God. You are a King's kid. You are royalty. You are greatness. You say these things to others, but do you honestly believe them?

I need you to believe them. I need you to communicate as though you fully understand and accept. I need you to operate from a space of abundance. I need you to flow from a space of overflow. I need you to flow as though you are the gift.

I need you to use a different word than "work" because it sets you in the space of force or requirement. What I have you doing isn't "work." It's operating in your gift, and it's a gift that people will be excited to compensate you handsomely for.

It's a gift I had given to many before you who were operating and carrying out my "work" in the world. Things will flow when you view this as a gift, not work. So effective today, see this as a gift (which it is), then permit yourself to flow in your gift fully.

Today will be unique. This week will be magical. These minor tweaks get you to the next breakthrough level to dive deeper into your internal growth. I love you."

Me: "Thank you, Lord, for speaking to me."

# Introduction

Y ou find yourself here, on the precipice of a profound journey inward. It's a journey born of the realization that answers to life's most significant questions often reside within the depths of your own being. You've traversed external landscapes, seeking knowledge and solace, only to discover that the most profound truths await your discovery within.

Perhaps you've played the role of the "strong friend," the dependable pillar of support for those around you. Yet, behind that strength lies the silent struggle of not putting yourself first, of prioritizing everyone else's needs above your own. You've sought solace in vacations, and brief respites from the demands of reality, but you know deep down that true transformation cannot be found in escape alone.

Now, you stand at the threshold of a life-altering journey, one that beckons you to reflect within, to rebuild and restore the wellspring of inner confidence that has long been neglected. You've given your all to solve, cure, heal, and uplift others, always placing yourself second in the process.

Over the next 21 days, you'll embark on a profound reprogramming of your inner narrative. It's a process that will allow you to reclaim your sense of self, to find safety and sanctuary within your own mind, body, and soul. This is your time to shift the paradigm, to recognize that self-care and self-love are not selfish acts but the foundation upon which your ability to help others truly thrives.

Embrace this journey with an open heart, for within the realms of self-discovery and self-compassion, you'll unearth the keys to living a life that honors your authenticity and nourishes your soul.

# What Is Forgiveness?

Forgiveness is accepting an apology that never came from your parents. Forgiveness is accepting an apology that never came from your parents. Your parents. They hurt you even though it wasn't on purpose. They. And you didn't deserve the things that happened to you. You know, a lot of times our parents, when you get in trouble, they'll be like, you deserved it.

But forgiveness is still accepting an apology that may never come. Forgiveness is that gift you're giving yourself to say, I've stayed here long enough. I've sat in this for too long. I won't allow this to torment me and hang over my head. I won't let the abuser have the power over me that I'm paralyzing.

The journey of forgiveness is a profound and transformative process that requires a deep wellspring of self-love. Before extending forgiveness to others, nurturing and cultivating a solid foundation of self-love within your heart is essential. Self-love serves as a powerful catalyst, enabling you to approach the act of forgiveness with authenticity, compassion, and a genuine desire for healing.

Forgiving yourself is a crucial initial step in this process. We often carry the weight of self-blame, regret, and guilt for our actions or perceived shortcomings. By practicing self-love, you create a safe and nurturing space within yourself to acknowledge your humanity, imperfections, and past mistakes.

# What It Is vs. What It Is Not

F orgiveness is a complex and deeply personal process that involves letting go of negative emotions and releasing the desire for revenge or punishment towards someone who has hurt, wronged, or disappointed you. It is a conscious choice to free yourself from resentment, anger, and bitterness, allowing you to move forward with your life more healthily and positively. Forgiveness is not about condoning or excusing the behavior of the person who hurt you; instead, it is a gift you give yourself to find peace and healing.

# What Forgiveness Is

## A Healing Process

Forgiveness is a powerful tool for healing emotional wounds. It can relieve the heavy emotional weight of holding onto grudges or resentment.

## A Choice

Forgiveness is a conscious decision to release negative feelings and replace them with compassion, understanding, and empathy. It involves actively choosing to let go of the pain and hurt.

## Empowerment

Forgiveness empowers you to take control of your emotions and reactions. It allows you to break free from the grip of the past and regain a sense of emotional well-being.

## Freedom

Forgiveness liberates you from the cycle of negativity. It enables you to break the chains that tie you to the person who hurt you and provides an opportunity to reclaim your emotional independence.

## Self-Love

Forgiveness is an act of self-love and self-care. It allows you to prioritize your well-being and mental health by releasing toxic emotions that can affect your overall quality of life.

# What Forgiveness Is Not

## Condoning or Excusing Behavior

Forgiving someone does not mean that you say their actions are acceptable or excusable. It's important to acknowledge that hurtful actions were wrong.

## Forgetting

Forgiving someone doesn't necessarily mean forgetting what happened. It's possible to forgive while remembering the past, as long as the memory doesn't continue to cause pain.

## Instantaneous

Forgiveness is a process that takes time. It doesn't always happen overnight, and it's okay to have conflicting emotions as you work through the process.

## Necessarily Reconciliation

Forgiving someone doesn't always mean you must reconcile with them or maintain a close relationship. You can forgive from a distance and still protect your boundaries.

## Weakness

Forgiveness is not a sign of weakness. It takes strength and courage to confront your emotions, work through them, and decide to forgive.

## Dependent on an Apology

While receiving an apology can facilitate the process, forgiveness is ultimately an internal journey you can undertake regardless of whether the person who hurt you apologizes or acknowledges their actions.

In essence, forgiveness is a transformative and liberating process that involves letting go of the past's emotional hold over you. It's a gift you give to yourself, allowing you to break free from the chains of anger and resentment and find greater peace, healing, and emotional freedom in your life.

# Story Time

Once upon a time, in a small, peaceful town, there lived a woman named Margaret. She had a daughter named Sarah, and their relationship was strained, to say the least. Margaret was carrying a heavy resentment and anger towards Sarah, but she refused to acknowledge it. She couldn't bring herself to admit that she was treating her daughter the same way her mother had treated her.

Years passed, and the divide between Margaret and Sarah grew wider. Sarah tried to reach out to mend the cracks in their relationship, but Margaret's pride and ego wouldn't allow it. She held onto her grudges like a shield, protecting her from the guilt and shame that lurked beneath the surface.

Sarah's wedding day came, which she had dreamt of sharing with her mother. But Margaret was not invited. It was a painful decision for Sarah, but she couldn't bear the thought of her mother's toxic presence tainting such a special day. Margaret never met her grandchildren, and the void in her heart grew each year.

As Margaret grew older, the weight of her unforgiveness became unbearable. She realized that her stubbornness had cost her the love of her daughter and the chance to know her grandchildren. It was time to heal, to mend the broken bonds of their family.

Margaret decided to take a step towards forgiveness. She purchased a journal titled "Forgiving Your Mother" and began to write. Each entry was a confession of her pain, guilt, and remorse. She poured her heart onto those pages, unearthing the deep-rooted emotions that had held her captive for so long.

It was a long and arduous journey, but Margaret was determined to change, to salvage what was left of her family. She knew it was never too late to start the healing process. As she continued to write and reflect, she hoped that one day, Sarah might find it in her heart to forgive her, and they could finally rebuild the relationship that had been shattered for far too long.

# Signs of Unforgiveness

U nforgiveness can be a heavy burden that silently affects various aspects of our lives. Recognizing the signs indicating you need to forgive is the first step towards healing and freeing yourself from resentment.

One clear indicator is the presence of tender emotions when the topic is discussed. If discussing the person or situation evokes strong emotions like sadness, hurt, or even anger, it's a sign that unresolved feelings linger beneath the surface.

Refusing to engage in vulnerable conversations is another signal. When you avoid discussing the issue or getting emotionally open about it, you may protect yourself from facing the pain associated with unforgiveness.

Anger and bitterness are common companions of unforgiveness. If you find yourself harboring intense anger or bitterness towards someone, it's a red flag that forgiveness is needed to release these toxic emotions.

Emotional checkout, where you disconnect from your feelings or become emotionally numb, can also indicate unforgiveness. It's a defense mechanism to avoid confronting painful emotions.

Feeling hindered or stagnated in a particular area of your life may result from unforgiveness. Holding onto grudges can block personal growth and progress.

Lastly, if mentioning the person's name triggers anger or resentment, it's a clear sign that unforgiveness still lingers in your heart.

Recognizing these signs is the first step towards the liberating journey of forgiveness, where you can find healing, emotional freedom, and inner peace.

# Story Time

Once upon a time in a quaint little town, there lived a woman named Hope. Despite her name, she struggled to find happiness in romantic relationships. She often blamed her father's absence during her childhood for her turbulent love life. Hope believed her "picker" was broken, as she seemed to choose the wrong men time and time again. Each relationship ended in heartache, and she carried the hurt from one into the next, making every man "pay" for the sins of his predecessors.

One day, Hope came across a journal titled "Forgiving Your Ex" by Tuniscia O. Intrigued, she decided to try it, hoping it might hold the answers she had been searching for. As she delved into the pages of the journal, Hope had a revelation that shook her to the core. It wasn't the men she had been angry with all these years; it was herself.

Hope realized she had been ignoring red flags and settling for less than she deserved because of her deep-seated fear of being alone. The root of her agony and pain stemmed from her childhood, from feeling neglected and unloved by her absent father. She had been seeking validation and love from these men, hoping they would fill the void left by her father's absence.

But as she continued to journal and reflect, Hope forgave herself. She acknowledged her worth and the strength it took to confront her past. She stopped looking for men to "fix" her and instead became her antidote and healer. Through self-love and acceptance, she began rebuilding her life, knowing she didn't need anyone else to complete her. With time, Hope found the happiness she had always sought within herself, and her once-broken picker began to guide her toward healthier, more fulfilling relationships.

# The Illusion of Forgiveness

Ignoring people is indeed distinct from forgiveness; it's a form of avoidance. While ignoring someone may temporarily shield you from uncomfortable emotions or interactions, it doesn't address the underlying issues that often necessitate forgiveness.

Forgiveness is a conscious and deliberate process of letting go of resentment, anger, or hurt from a past offense or wrongdoing. It involves acknowledging the pain and emotions associated with the situation, understanding them, and choosing to release them. Forgiveness doesn't mean condoning the actions of the person who hurt you; rather, it's about freeing yourself from the emotional burden and finding closure.

On the other hand, ignoring someone can lead to unresolved conflicts and emotional baggage. It may create an atmosphere of tension and unease, both within yourself and in your relationships. Ignoring someone doesn't provide the healing and resolution that forgiveness can offer.

It's important to note that forgiveness doesn't necessarily require direct interaction with the person who hurt you. It can be a personal journey of letting go, finding inner peace, and moving forward. However, it involves consciously addressing and processing your feelings rather than simply avoiding them. Ultimately, forgiveness is a powerful tool for your emotional well-being and growth, while ignoring people can hinder your ability to heal and thrive fully.

# Cultivating Self-Compassion

Cultivating self-compassion is a transformative journey that leads to profound personal growth and emotional well-being. It begins with the realization that you are your best friend; as such, you deserve the same love, patience, and understanding that you readily extend to others.

Remember that these are opportunities for self-compassion to shine in moments of self-doubt or when you revisit past mistakes. Instead of harsh self-criticism, offer yourself words of encouragement and support. Acknowledge that you are a work in progress, just like everyone else, and that missteps are an integral part of the human experience.

As you nurture self-compassion, you'll find that your inner dialogue becomes a wellspring of positivity and resilience. You'll be better equipped to face challenges with a sense of self-assuredness and a deep well of self-love. Your relationship with yourself will transform, becoming a source of strength and comfort.

So, embrace self-compassion as a daily practice. Write down your self-love affirmations in your journal, reminding yourself of your inherent worthiness. Treat yourself with the kindness and understanding you would offer to a cherished friend, and watch as this practice enriches your life, leading to a deeper sense of fulfillment and inner peace.

# Embracing Imperfections

Embracing imperfections is a profound act of self-acceptance and personal growth. It's a recognition that perfection is an unattainable ideal and that the beauty of life lies in its imperfections.

Your imperfections are not shortcomings but facets of your character that make you unique. They are the brushstrokes on the canvas of your life, creating a rich tapestry of experiences and growth. Instead of viewing mistakes and flaws as failures, see them as opportunities for learning and self-improvement.

By embracing imperfections, you free yourself from unrealistic expectations and self-criticism. You allow room for self-compassion and self-love to flourish. When you accept your imperfections, you become more resilient in facing challenges, knowing that setbacks are part of the journey toward self-discovery and personal evolution.

In your journal, reflect on your imperfections and the valuable lessons they have brought into your life. Write about the growth and wisdom you've gained from your mistakes. As you embrace your imperfections, you'll find a greater sense of peace, self-assuredness, and the freedom to be yourself authentically. Remember, it's the cracks in the facade that let the light in, and it's your imperfections that make you beautifully human.

# Releasing Self-Judgment

Releasing self-judgment is an act of self-compassion that can profoundly impact your well-being and daily life. Often, we are our own harshest critics, dwelling on perceived shortcomings and mistakes, which can lead to feelings of guilt and unworthiness.

In your journal, create a space where you actively challenge and replace self-judgment with self-affirmation. Acknowledge your efforts, no matter how small they may seem. Write about your progress on your journey of self-forgiveness and healing. Remind yourself of your innate goodness and worthiness.

By releasing self-judgment, you free yourself from negative self-talk and create a more nurturing inner dialogue. This shift in perspective can boost your self-esteem, reduce anxiety, and improve your overall mental and emotional well-being.

As you journal about releasing self-judgment, you'll discover that self-compassion is a powerful force for self-forgiveness and personal growth. It allows you to approach each day with a sense of kindness and understanding, not only for others but, most importantly, for yourself.

# Setting Boundaries with Your Inner Critic

Setting boundaries with your inner critic is a profound act of self-love and self-compassion. The inner critic can be relentless, filling your mind with self-doubt and negativity. Recognizing that this critical voice is not an accurate reflection of your worth or potential is essential.

Create a dedicated space to address and challenge your inner critic in your journal. When self-doubt arises, counter it with affirmations of your inherent value and your capacity for growth. Remind yourself of your unique strengths and qualities. Write about your past achievements and successes, no matter how small they may seem.

You establish a protective shield around your self-esteem and well-being by setting boundaries with your inner critic. You refuse to let self-doubt and negativity define your self-worth. Instead, you empower yourself to cultivate self-love and self-acceptance.

As you continue this practice in your journal, you'll find that your inner critic's voice diminishes, allowing self-compassion and self-forgiveness to flourish. This transformation allows you to approach life with greater confidence and resilience, knowing that you deserve love and kindness from yourself just as much as from others.

# Practicing Self-Forgiveness

Practicing self-forgiveness is a powerful and transformative journey that you can embark upon through journaling. In your journal, engage in a deliberate act of self-forgiveness by writing a heartfelt letter to yourself.

In this letter, start by acknowledging the mistakes and choices you've made in the past that have caused you pain or regret. Allow yourself to express genuine remorse for these actions or decisions. It's essential to be honest and compassionate with yourself during this process, recognizing that being human means making mistakes.

As you pour your feelings onto the pages of your journal, you begin the process of releasing pent-up emotions. This cathartic experience can be incredibly healing, allowing you to confront and process any guilt, shame, or self-blame that may have been holding you back.

Ultimately, self-forgiveness is an act of self-compassion. By offering forgiveness to yourself, you free yourself from the chains of the past and open the door to self-healing and growth. Through this practice, you can nurture a kinder and more forgiving relationship with yourself, paving the way for a brighter and more empowered future.

# Prioritizing Self-Care

Prioritizing self-care is an essential component of your journey toward self-forgiveness and self-compassion. It's a deliberate and loving act towards yourself that can profoundly impact your overall well-being.

Self-care encompasses a wide range of activities and practices designed to nurture your physical, emotional, and mental health. It can be as simple as taking a few moments each day to practice deep breathing or meditation to calm your mind. Alternatively, it can involve engaging in activities you love, whether pursuing a hobby, spending time in nature, or reading a book that brings you joy.

Spending quality time with supportive friends and loved ones can also be a form of self-care. These connections provide emotional support and remind you that you are valued and loved.

Mindfulness, or being fully present in the moment, is another powerful tool for self-care. It can help you cultivate self-awareness and self-compassion by allowing you to observe your thoughts and feelings without judgment.

Incorporating self-care into your daily routine reinforces your self-worth and self-love. It's a way of saying to yourself that you deserve to be treated with kindness and respect, starting with how you treat yourself. By prioritizing self-care, you take proactive steps to heal, grow, and nurture a deeper sense of self-forgiveness and self-compassion.

# Visualizing Your Healing

Visualizing your healing is a powerful practice that can guide you on your journey of self-forgiveness and self-compassion. It allows you to see yourself not as a victim of your past mistakes but as a resilient and empowered individual capable of transformation.

Close your eyes and imagine a version of yourself free from the burdens of guilt and self-blame. Visualize this healed version of you as radiant, confident, and at peace with your past. Picture yourself standing tall, your heart filled with self-compassion and forgiveness, and your spirit vibrant with self-love.

As you visualize your healing, focus on the emotions accompanying this transformation – a sense of lightness, freedom from judgment, and an overwhelming feeling of self-acceptance. Imagine how these emotions radiate from you, positively impacting your relationships and overall well-being.

Visualizing your healing is not about denying your past mistakes or experiences but about recognizing your capacity to grow and evolve beyond them. It's a reminder that you have the inner strength and resilience to overcome challenges and emerge as a stronger, more compassionate version of yourself.

Regularly practicing this visualization reinforces your commitment to self-forgiveness and self-compassion. It serves as a guiding light, helping you stay on the path toward healing and personal growth.

## Expressing Gratitude for Yourself

Expressing gratitude for yourself is a transformative practice that fosters self-love and self-acceptance. It's acknowledging your worth and the unique qualities that make you who you are.

Take a moment each day to reflect on your strengths and achievements. Consider the challenges you've overcome, the skills you've developed, and the personal growth you've experienced. Express gratitude for these aspects of yourself, recognizing that they contribute to your overall well-being.

Additionally, acknowledge the positive qualities that define you. Are you compassionate, resilient, creative, or empathetic? These traits are part of what makes you a remarkable individual. Embrace them and express gratitude for the positive impact they have on your life and the lives of those around you.

When you express gratitude for yourself, you shift your focus from self-criticism to self-appreciation. It reminds you that you deserve love and kindness, both from others and yourself. This practice can boost your self-esteem and self-confidence, paving the way for a deeper sense of self-worth.

Incorporate this practice into your daily routine by journaling or simply reflecting on your positive qualities and achievements. As you consistently express gratitude for yourself, you'll cultivate a stronger and more positive relationship with the most important person in your life – yourself.

As you embrace self-love and work towards forgiving yourself, you'll find that extending forgiveness to others becomes more authentic and heart-centered. By understanding your worthiness of forgiveness, you pave the way for a deeper, more compassionate connection with those you seek to forgive. Self-love becomes the bridge that leads you from a place of hurt and resentment to a place of genuine healing, reconciliation, and growth.

# Unmask The Control Disguised As Caring

Unmasking the control disguised as caring is a profound journey of self-awareness and empowerment. Often, control can masquerade as concern or protection in various aspects of our lives. Recognizing this hidden control is the first step toward breaking free, whether it's in personal relationships, work dynamics, or even within ourselves.

In personal relationships, control may manifest as an overwhelming need to dictate every aspect of a loved one's life while safeguarding their well-being. It can stifle individuality and independence, hindering personal growth and autonomy. Unmasking this control requires honest introspection and a commitment to fostering trust and respect in the relationship.

In the workplace, control can take the form of micromanagement, limiting creativity and innovation. It may stem from a fear of losing control or a desire for perfection. Acknowledging this control allows for a more collaborative and productive work environment where employees can contribute their unique skills and ideas.

Lastly, the most challenging aspect can be recognizing control within ourselves. Sometimes, we impose strict expectations and limitations on our lives, believing it to be self-care or discipline. Unmasking this self-imposed control enables us to embrace self-compassion, allowing for personal growth and a healthier sense of self.

In all these areas, unmasking control is a courageous act that leads to greater freedom, authenticity, and the ability to foster healthier, more nurturing relationships with others and ourselves.

# What Journaling Means To Me

Journaling is my daily refuge, a sacred practice woven into the tapestry of my life. It's a lifeline that has steadied me through the stormy seas of emotional turmoil. When I found myself trapped in the suffocating grip of a functioning depression, journaling threw me a lifeline.

As the sun gently kissed the world awake each morning, I poured my heart onto the pages. These blank sheets, like a compassionate friend, held my darkest thoughts and deepest fears without judgment.

In the depths of despair, when quitting seemed like the only option, my journal whispered words of hope and resilience. It became my confidant, absorbing the tears and doubts that threatened to consume me. It was there as I watched my children grapple with insurmountable challenges. I chronicled their struggles and victories, finding solace in bearing witness to their journeys.

But journaling is more than a refuge; it's a dialogue with the divine. Amidst the chaos of life, I engage in daily conversations with God. I ask questions, seeking guidance and understanding. Sometimes, in the hush of those moments, I hear His whispers of wisdom, gently illuminating my path.

My journal is a treasure trove of experiences, emotions, and revelations. It's a testament to my resilience, a record of my evolution. Journaling is my pillar of strength, a companion on this rollercoaster ride called life.

It's not just a habit; it's an integral part of who I am—a testament to the healing power of self-expression and self-reflection.

Journaling is not a religious practice but a mindful connection within. It transcends faith boundaries, offering a sacred space for self-reflection, healing, and personal growth. Regardless of one's beliefs, journaling serves as a universal tool to explore the depths of the human experience and foster inner understanding.

Over the next 21 days, I share my sacred entries with you in the hope that they may offer solace and inspiration on your journey.

# PART 1

## FORGIVENESS

## FREE YOUR MIND, BODY & SOUL

*DAY 1*

# ACKNOWLEDGE YOUR PAIN &
# HOW IT'S HOLDING YOU BACK

**Forgiveness Thought of the Day**

Today, I explore the profound power of acknowledging my pain as the first step toward healing emotional wounds. I understand that acknowledging my pain doesn't mean I deserved it or that I must swiftly forgive and forget. Instead, it's about granting myself the permission to be honest, to accept that someone or something has caused me hurt, and that this pain continues to affect me emotionally or mentally.

In this process, I'm creating a safe space within myself, a sanctuary where I can shine a gentle light on those tender parts I've carefully tucked away to shield myself from further harm. It's an act of courage to go inward, to acknowledge the wounds that have been silently shaping my inner landscape.

I also recognize that not everyone will comprehend my emotional struggles, and that's perfectly okay. This journey is a deeply personal one, and I am the tenderhearted friend I've longed for. I need my understanding, my empathy, and my compassion now more than ever.

So, as I take this first step toward healing, I know that I'm not alone. By acknowledging my pain, I begin the transformative journey of self-compassion and emotional restoration, paving the way for a brighter, more resilient future.

**Meditative Reflection "Word of the Day"**

## MY JOURNAL ENTRY

### September 15, 2022

### Words of the Day: "I Love You."

"Today, the words "I LOVE YOU" floated in during my morning meditation.

These words are filled with adoration and sometimes laced with manipulation.

I appreciate how I look in the mirror to admire my beautiful face smiling back at me—the reflection of wisdom in my eyes, which have carried me gracefully through every battle and victory.

The loyalty of my body shows up daily to perform.

Growing up, I learned to say, "I love you" to others.

Yet, the most profound connection of love needs to be a gift I gave to myself before sharing it with others.

I need my love. I need my acknowledgment. I always get to love myself.

When I disappoint others, I'm still lovable. When I make mistakes, love is still available to me.

When I lie to myself, self-love will reconnect me to my truth.

My love is a vehicle to drive me toward rejuvenation.

Self-love is a safe space of refuge when negative thoughts try to consume me.

My love is a muscle requiring constant exercise to build its strength.

My love is an automatic reflex when touched in the right spot.

My love is always ready to show up.

Love will also sit on the sidelines when it's not requested.

Love is a gentle force of power. Love can wash away all sorrow.

Love is a connection to my soul. Love is a friend until the days of old.

Love is a constant companion. Love nurtures. Love is shared through a smile. Love is wrapped in a warm hug.

Love is reflected in the stars. Love is heard as the waves crash on the beach.

Love is a call to say, "I apologize. I miss you. Please forgive me."

Love is reconnection. Love is restoration. Love has healthy boundaries.

Love is clarity. Love is unity. Love is wholeness. Love is euphoric.

Love is present even in sorrow. Love is happiness. Love is generational healing.

Love is telling the truth.

Love is my reflection in the mirror.

Love knows when to quit. Love is moving past the obstacles.

Love is accepting blessings. Love is expecting miracles. Love is embracing the favor.

Love has faith.

Self-love coupled with inner trust is taking action even when it feels scary.

Love is belief. Love is courage. Love is consistency. Love is what I decide.

Love is introspective. Love is a gift. My love is felt in every moment.

Self-love is savoring a shared memory from the past. Love is energy.

Love is always looking for me.

Therefore, I will always be my first love, feeling my love, experiencing my love, embodying my passion, and receiving love.

Self-love is the greatest gift of all. Thank you. I love you.

**Deeper Connection Within**

1. How has your fear of being in love with your authentic self held you back?

_____

_____

_____

_____

2. What areas in your life are you "invisible" to stay safe and accepted?

_____

_____

_____

_____

_____

3. Who will you become when you embrace self-love?

_____

_____

_____

_____

_____

**Gratitude Reflection of the Day**

Today, I am grateful for the opportunity to forgive myself, acknowledging that I am a work in progress and self-compassion is key to my growth.

**Forgiveness Exercise of the Day:**

Write yourself a Love Letter:

_____

_____

_____

_____

_____

_____

_____

_____

_____

_____

_____

_____

_____

_____

_____

_____

_____

_____

_____

_____

_____

_____

_____

_____

*DAY 2*

# DECLUTTER EMOTIONS FORGIVE THE OFFENSE. LEARN THE LESSON. RELEASE IT

**Forgiveness Thought of the Day**

Today, I contemplate the power of decluttering my emotions. Just as we tidy our physical spaces, cleaning up our emotional world is equally crucial. When was the last time I cleared my emotional closet, making space for positivity? I'll start by sweeping away negative self-talk, banishing the specter of fear, and acknowledging my secret struggles.

By decluttering limiting beliefs and organizing my thoughts, I pave the way for transformative change. Dreams once obscured by the chaos of emotional clutter now gleam brightly, ready to be pursued.

As I get honest with myself, I invite inner peace and self-acceptance. My life will transform profoundly as I release the burdens of the past and create space for forgiveness. I will emerge lighter, freer, and more resilient. Clarity will replace confusion, and the light of understanding will illuminate my path forward.

Decluttering emotions is an act of self-love, a commitment to personal growth, and an embrace of the forgiveness journey. By reorganizing my thoughts and decluttering my emotional space, I unlock the door to a life filled with greater purpose, joy, and authenticity.

**Meditative Reflection "Word of the Day"**

## MY JOURNAL ENTRY

## September 7, 2022

## Word of the Day: "Accountability"

"Breathe in and breathe out.

Reflecting on my actions and decisions to make others comfortable, I realize my desire to be "nice" or harmonious sometimes supersedes my ability to be clear and direct.

I can be kindhearted and direct while following my intuition.

Inner trust and accountability outweigh my desire to please others.

I get to own my truth without worrying whether people will accept me.

I welcome the idea of taking bold actions even when others lack the faith to believe. And I align my habits with my dreams.

I'm leaving the past behind as I stretch to grow.

No matter what life hands me, I am always accountable for responding, reacting, and navigating forward.

## Deeper Connection Within

1. What secret emotional clutter is holding you back?

_____

_____

_____

_____

_____

2. What areas of your life are you ready to declutter, and who will you become due to this action?

_____

_____

_____

_____

_____

3. I forgive myself, and I permit myself to release_____

_____so I can welcome

_____ in my life.

## Gratitude Reflection of the Day

I'm thankful for the moments when I appreciate myself, recognizing my unique qualities and the value I bring to the world.

**Exercise of the Day:**

It's <u>One Year</u> from now.

Write a letter to yourself sharing <u>Your Accomplishments</u> due to <u>Your Accountability</u>.

_____

_____

_____

_____

_____

_____

_____

_____

_____

_____

_____

_____

_____

_____

_____

_____

_____

_____

_____

_____

# Explore/Find Source of Pain

## Forgiveness Thought of the Day

Today, I reflect on the journey of forgiveness and the importance of exploring the source of my pain. It's crucial to clarify my intentions in this process. I'm not here to 'fix' myself, to 'ignore' the past, or to wallow in guilt over past perceived failures.

Instead, I aim to engage in a thoughtful and compassionate exploration of my pain. I acknowledge it without judgment, understanding that it's a natural part of the human experience. By identifying the roots of my pain, I shine a light on the shadows that have shaped my emotions.

Furthermore, I recognize the significance of understanding my emotional triggers. What stirs these feelings of hurt, resentment, or guilt? Exploring these triggers allows me to unravel the complexities of my emotional landscape and gain greater self-awareness.

Through this process, I'm not dwelling on the past but learning from it. I'm not dwelling on my failures but seeking growth opportunities. I'm not trying to change who I am but striving to evolve into the best version of myself.

Today, I commit to acknowledging and identifying my pain and emotional triggers. I choose to take these steps forward with a heart full of compassion, embracing the transformative power of forgiveness on my journey toward healing and self-discovery.

**Meditative Reflection "Word of the Day"**

**MY JOURNAL ENTRY**

**September 11, 2022**

**Word of the Day: "Ease"**

"Breathe in. Breathe out with ease.

Today, during my meditation, ease was the word that stood out.

Flowers grow with ease. I am blessed to walk with ease. Money is magnetized to me with ease. I adore my husband with ease.

Clients are attracted to me with ease. People pay me with ease. My laughter flows with ease. I forgive myself with ease. I forgive others with ease (this one took practice).

I release "it" with ease. I grow forward with ease. I connect to soul alignments with ease. I am acknowledging my greatness with ease. I appreciate myself with ease.

I am selling products with ease. I accept my children's decisions easily. Favorable responses flow with ease.

I am celebrating life with ease. I cherish myself with ease. I complete marathons with ease.

I am writing creatively with ease. I manifest wealth with ease. I welcome a luxurious life with ease. I receive abundance with ease. Money flows to me with ease.

I am saving money with ease. I purchase investment properties with ease. I feel safe with money with ease. I make wise financial decisions with ease. I hire the perfect employees with ease.

I am a confident CEO with ease. I am a gentle friend with ease. I forgive my mother with ease. I listen to learn with ease. I listen to understand with ease.

I am listening to hear my inner soul with ease. I am listening to reconnect with others with ease.

I am listening to my intuition with ease. I am listening to God's instructions with ease. I am focusing on one thing at a time with ease. I care about people with ease.

I discuss money with ease. I raise my prices with ease. I am paid with ease. I am setting boundaries with ease.

Being playful with ease. Rejoicing with ease. Celebrating others with ease. Navigating beyond my discomfort with ease.

Accepting differences with ease. Respecting people's boundaries with ease. Listening without judgment with ease. Watching without judgment with ease. Moving on with ease.

Being misunderstood with ease. Eating healthy with ease. Sitting in silence with ease. Embracing stillness with ease. Exercising with ease. Writing books with ease.

Embracing my weaknesses with ease. Releasing people, places, and things that no longer serve me with ease.

I love myself with ease. I allow people to appreciate me with ease. I trust people with ease. I trust myself with ease. I speak positively to myself with ease.

I am taking accountability for my life with ease. I stopped overly explaining myself with ease. I say "no" with ease. I am minding my business with ease.

Speaking up for myself with ease. Putting myself first with ease. Being confident with ease. Enjoying a luxurious life with ease. Asking for what I want with ease.

Admiring all of me with ease. Seizing the moment with ease. Knowing I belong with ease. Asking for more with ease. Stepping back with ease.

Restoring connections with ease. Embracing healthy relationships with ease. Accepting the apology then my setting boundaries with ease.

Restoring my soul with ease. Forgiving myself with ease. Exploring new things with ease. Being corrected with ease. Making mistakes with ease. Taking the journey alone with ease.

Starting the new business venture with ease. Accepting "no" with ease. Celebrating my victories with ease. Celebrating myself with ease. Changing my mind with ease.

Saying "yes" when no one else understands with ease.

I decide if it's easy or difficult. Hard things are hard, but when my mindset is determined to focus on the ease within the journey, it will always create space for miracles to appear all around.

## Deeper Connection Within

I forgive myself, and I will no longer suffocate my mind with judgments of _____
_____
_____.

I forgive myself and will no longer settle for struggling to receive the approval of_____
_____for
_____
_____.

I forgive myself and move forward with tenderness and self-acceptance to fully treasure all parts of me from the inside out.

## Gratitude Reflection of the Day

I appreciate the love I extend to myself, knowing that self-love is the foundation of a fulfilling and joyful life.

**Forgiveness Exercise of the Day:**

It's <u>One Year</u> from now.

Write a letter to yourself about how WELCOMING EASE has transformed your life.

_____

_____

_____

_____

_____

_____

_____

_____

_____

_____

_____

_____

_____

_____

_____

_____

_____

_____

_____

_____

_____

_____

# DAY 4

# Identify Triggers

**Forgiveness Thought of the Day**

"Today, I dive deep into the exploration of forgiveness, focusing on the significance of identifying triggers and taking accountability for my responses. It's an essential part of my journey towards healing and self-growth.

Reflecting on the past, I recognize that certain situations or words can act as emotional triggers, evoking strong reactions within me. Instead of suppressing or avoiding these triggers, I confront them with curiosity and self-awareness.

Identifying triggers is not about assigning blame or dwelling on past wounds. It's about understanding the patterns that shape my emotional responses. Doing so allows me greater control over my reactions and paves the way for healthier interactions.

Moreover, accountability plays a pivotal role in this process. I acknowledge that I can choose how I respond to triggers. It's a conscious decision to respond with empathy, compassion, and understanding, even in emotional turmoil.

Today, I embrace the transformative power of self-awareness and accountability. I commit to identifying triggers, understanding their origins, and taking responsibility for my responses. In doing so, I empower myself to navigate the challenges of forgiveness with grace and resilience."

**Meditative Reflection "Word of the Day"**

## MY JOURNAL ENTRY

### September 29, 2022

### Words of the Day: "I Accept Life As It Is"

"Breathe in. Breathe out. In today's mediation, "I accept life as it is" flowed to me.

A calm peace flowed over me as I repeated the mantra.

It is a "knowingness" of everything as it should be in the moment.

Nothing is added, taken away, or wished for differently because this moment is inevitable. This moment right now is precious.

Staying present right now, mind, body, and soul radiates empowerment. Right now is all I have—this moment.

Focusing on right now connects me deeper with my intuition.

Being present requires me to surrender instead of creating illusions of what could have, should have, and would have been if only things were a little different.

I accept people as they are and take accountability for my boundaries. I accept my responsibility to shift to create different outcomes in the future. I accept all of me.

I get life as it is. I acknowledge that my business is where it is due to my daily habits.

I accept high vibrational energy. I accept delightful moments and treasure them.

I accept and nurture my tender parts within. I receive forgiveness and always welcome it into my life. I accept people as they are and take accountability for who I include in my inner circle.

I accept money and invite it affectionately into my life. I accept my body and express gratitude for all it does to keep me healthy.

I accept corrections because I will make mistakes. I accept my weaknesses and use them to help me grow. I accept rejection as a part of life. I accept success. I accept mistakes will happen and welcome lessons learned.

I accept miracles cause they are always around me. I accept misunderstandings are unavoidable. I welcome marvelous gifts. I accept open doors when they lead to my desired destination.

I accept closed doors because something better is on its way. I accept the favor. I accept blessings and receive them with an open heart. I accept divine connections with a grateful heart. I always accept peaceful resolutions.

I accept all of me just as I am.

I accept past decisions and forgive myself for those who caused me hardship, and I am celebrating all the ones that brought me happiness.

I am accountable for my actions and reactions.

## Deeper Connection Within

1. What habits or behaviors make you feel guilty or ashamed but continue doing them to please someone else?

_____

_____

_____

_____

_____

2. What inner parts crave more of your tenderness?

_____

_____

_____

_____

_____

3. How has your fear of rejection held you back?

_____

_____

_____

_____

_____

## Gratitude Reflection of the Day

Today, I send kind and thankful thoughts to myself, affirming my worthiness and the beauty of my journey.

**Forgiveness Exercise of the Day:**

It's <u>One Year</u> from now.

Write a letter to yourself sharing how YOUR LIFE TRANSFORMED once you ACCEPTED LIFE AS IT IS and stopped focusing on the past.

_____

_____

_____

_____

_____

_____

_____

_____

_____

_____

_____

_____

_____

_____

_____

_____

_____

_____

_____

_____

_____

# Unforgiveness Only Impacts You

## Forgiveness Thought of the Day

"Today's Forgiveness Reflection centers on the profound truth that unforgiveness primarily affects me. It's a reminder to silence the noise of bitterness and disappointment that can often overwhelm my thoughts.

When dwelling on past hurts or disappointments, I acknowledge that these thoughts can create a heavy burden within me. They don't harm the individuals or situations I hold grievances against as much as they affect my emotional well-being.

In those moments, I choose to be mindful of the noise these thoughts generate. Instead of letting them fester, I actively intervene with encouragement and positive affirmations. I remind myself that holding onto grudges or resentments only hinders my growth and inner peace.

I regain control over my emotional state by silencing the negative noise and replacing it with affirmations of self-love and forgiveness. I understand that forgiveness is a gift I give to myself, liberating me from the shackles of the past.

Today, I commit to nurturing my inner peace by choosing forgiveness over bitterness. I recognize that the noise of unforgiveness only impacts me, and I choose to silence it with words of self-compassion and positivity."

## Meditative Reflection "Word of the Day"

### MY JOURNAL ENTRY

### September 9, 2022

### Words of the Day: "Positive Light"

Breathe in. Breathe out.

A positive light is all around me, filling a room with laughter. It's a sweet smile on the face of a stranger. A friendly "hello" while walking.

A silent moment while staring out of the window. A mother's gentle prayer for her children.

Playful thoughts. Intentional connections. Peaceful ideas to prosper. Tenderhearted energy to help a stranger. A gentle smile when it all comes together.

The excitement for a job well done. The celebration of unity and connection. The alignment of happiness and gratitude. The appreciation in precious moments.

The acceptance felt when surrounded by loved ones. The acknowledgment of inner wisdom. The acceptance of inner peace. The confidence of self-trust. The happiness of achieving goals.

The delight of magic happening in my life. The lightheartedness of making a new friend. The playfulness of taking the first step. The belief in miraculous outcomes.

The faith to believe the best. The confidence to start over. The inner peace of forgiving myself. The gift of forgiving others.

The tranquility of letting go and moving on. The humility of saying, "I apologize."

The inner connection to accept all of you. The feeling of the sun kissing your skin. The adrenaline of completing a workout. The excitement of a new adventure.

The curiosity of exploring the world through blissful eyes. The magic of seeing a miracle. The warmth of a hug. The thankfulness to have people to celebrate you.

Positive light is everywhere, always playful in my presence.

See it. Feel it. Find it. Receive it. Embrace it. Acknowledge it, for it's always ready to brighten my day and expose the magic all around.

## Deeper Connection Within

I will no longer be tortured by thoughts of _____

_____

I choose to forgive _____
_____, and my forgiveness does not mean

_____
_____ it just means I am free to

_____
_____ with my life.

## Gratitude Reflection of the Day

I'm grateful for the confidence I am building within myself, realizing that it empowers me to pursue my dreams and aspirations.

**Forgiveness Exercise of the Day:**

It's <u>Three Months</u> from now.

Write a letter to yourself sharing how focusing on YOUR POSITIVE LIGHT is helping you heal.

_____

_____

_____

_____

_____

_____

_____

_____

_____

_____

_____

_____

_____

_____

_____

_____

_____

_____

_____

_____

_____

_____

_____

_____

_____

_____

_____

_____

_____

_____

_____

_____

_____

_____

_____

_____

_____

_____

_____

_____

_____

_____

_____

_____

_____I am a light in my life.

# I Didn't Deserve It

## Forgiveness Thought of the Day

Today's Forgiveness Thought of the Day brings to light a powerful truth: sometimes, we find ourselves in situations where we didn't deserve the pain or hurt that came our way. It's a part of life's unpredictable journey.

Throughout our lives, we've been conditioned to assign blame or take responsibility when damage is done. However, a crucial aspect often goes unaddressed - the process of healing once the storm has passed.

It's essential to acknowledge that you may not have caused the pain, and you certainly didn't deserve it. But here's the transformative insight: healing is your responsibility. It's about taking your power back.

Instead of expending all your energy on pointing fingers or dwelling on who's at fault, redirect your focus toward something equally important - your happiness and well-being. Consider what could happen if you consciously prioritize your healing and happiness.

By shifting your perspective from blame to personal empowerment, you pave the way for profound transformation. You become the architect of your emotional well-being, transcending the constraints of past pain and opening yourself up to the possibility of genuine happiness.

Today, I embrace the responsibility of my healing journey, recognizing that I may not have deserved the pain, but I certainly deserve to be happy.

**Meditative Reflection "Word of the Day"**

## MY JOURNAL ENTRY

### October 3, 2022

### Word of the Day: "Tenderness"

Breathe in. Breathe out.

Today, during my meditation, the word tenderness floated into my space.

Tears welled in my eyes as I reflected on all the situations where tenderness resuscitated me. After a mistake:

1. Offer myself tenderness.

2. Let tenderness be the guide while thinking of my shattered parts within.

3. I forgive myself and others as I heal my emotional suffering.

My father, who didn't know how to value me, needs tenderness.

My mother, who betrayed me, requires my tender thoughts for me to heal and reconnect.

Welcome tenderness when negative self-talk starts to creep in.

When I say "yes" but need to say no, I must be tender with myself and curious about the pattern.

When I quit on myself, tenderness will lead me back to self-confidence.

Tenderness is a guiding light to mend my inner wounds. Tenderness is gentleness. Sprinkle tenderness on my tongue before I respond.

Include tenderness in my thoughts, actions, and habits.

Situations have happened to me that I did not deserve. Use tenderness, grace, forgiveness, and boundaries to help empower me to move forward.

## Deeper Connection Within

I am unplugging my emotional attachment to _____

_____.

I forgive myself, and I am deciding to release the mental and emotional torment of_____

_____

_____. I did not deserve it.

Releasing it simply means I choose to no longer allow the hurtful memories of_____

_____

_to have power over me. I am taking my energy back.

## Gratitude Reflection of the Day

I appreciate the times when I forgive my past mistakes, understanding that they were opportunities for growth and learning.

**Forgiveness Exercise of the Day:**

Look in the mirror and repeat this:

I deserve to heal.

I deserve to forgive myself.

I deserve to smile again.

I deserve to trust myself again.

I deserve to be loved again.

I deserve to be surrounded by people who love and care about me.

I deserve to have what you want.

I deserve forgiveness.

I deserve to put myself first.

I deserve authenticity.

I deserve healthy relationships.

Although you can't change the past, you deserve to create a blissful future, and only YOU can do it.

Then, take a moment to journal what you experienced.

# Inner Reflection

*DAY 7*

# Receive the Gift of Self-Forgiveness

## Forgiveness Thought of the Day

"Today's Forgiveness Reflection of the Day resonates deeply with me as it speaks of the precious gift of self-forgiveness. This gift, the very first one we encounter when entering the serene garden of forgiveness, is one to be held close and cherished.

Imagine it as a beautifully wrapped present, and as we open it, we discover the keys that unlock the doors to our future. These keys represent the transformative power of self-forgiveness.

Self-forgiveness is a cornerstone of personal growth and healing. It liberates us from the burdens of our past, freeing us from the chains of guilt, shame, and regret. When we embrace self-forgiveness, we open the door to self-compassion and self-acceptance, allowing us to truly understand our own humanity.

With these keys, we can navigate our inner landscape with greater ease, fostering a sense of wholeness and self-worth. As we hug this gift tight and cherish it, we embark on a journey toward a future filled with light, healing, and endless possibilities.

Today, I celebrate the gift of self-forgiveness and the incredible potential it holds for shaping a brighter and more fulfilling future."

**Meditative Reflection "Word of the Day"**

## MY JOURNAL ENTRY
### September 10, 2022
### Word of the Day: "Possibilities"

Breathe in. Breathe out. Possibilities

As I meditated this morning, possibilities flowed through my mind.

The idea of infinite possibilities in every area of my life excites me. Possibilities for massive favor. Possibilities for miraculous connections.

Possibilities for an abundance of wealth to flow into my life. Possibilities for my life to shift abundantly at any second.

Possibilities for instant connections. Possibilities for the magic to happen right now. Possibilities for me to gift transformation to others.

Possibilities for me to share jubilant moments with strangers. Possibilities for me to give generational gifts. Possibilities for me to change the world.

Possibilities for me to magnetize billions. Possibilities for me to engage with global leaders. Possibility for me to magnetize a new home this year.

Possibilities for me to run marathons while having fun. Possibilities for me to always travel the world luxuriously. Possibilities for me to live a first-class life.

Possibilities for me to magnetize daily blissfulness. Possibilities for me to attract happy people to me. Possibilities for me to restore trusting relationships.

Possibilities for me to enjoy jubilant friendships. Possibilities for me to magnetize corporate connections and sponsorships. Possibilities for me to consistently engage in healthy communication.

Possibility for me to carry positive energy. Possibilities to magnetize wealth with ease. Possibilities for me to magnetize tens of millions this year.

Possibilities for me to attract the perfect employees. Possibilities for me to always be confident in business decisions.

Possibilities for my nervous system to feel safe with money. Possibilities for my nervous system to feel safe with abundant wealth. Possibilities for me to have a healthy body as I get older.

Possibilities for me to expect happy outcomes. Possibilities for me to continually receive God's divine favor. Possibilities for me to embody wholeness.

Believing what I am searching for is searching for me, too.

The world has infinite possibilities, and I welcome supernatural manifestations.

And so it is.

**Deeper Connection Within**

I apologize to myself for _____
_____
_____.

I appreciate how I _____
_____
_____.

I am grateful for my _____
_____
_____.

**Gratitude Reflection of the Day**

I appreciate the times when I forgive my past mistakes, understanding that they were opportunities for growth and learning.

**Forgiveness Exercise of the Day:**

Write a letter to yourself welcoming all of the POSSIBILITIES into your life.

_____

_____

_____

_____

_____

_____

_____

_____

_____

_____

_____

_____

_____

_____

_____

_____

_____

_____

_____

_____

_____

_____

*PART II*

**HEAL**

**Your Soul Knows What It Needs**

# Release The Mental Torment

## Forgiveness Thought of the Day

Today's Forgiveness Thought of the Day brings a profound realization: preserving our energy by letting go of the need to change others. It's a lesson that resonates deeply with me as I reflect on the mental torment often accompanying the desire to prove our point and make someone else wrong.

In life, we encounter situations where people may intentionally do things to provoke or annoy us. It's a natural response to want to set things right, to make them see our perspective, and to rectify the situation. However, this can become a draining and futile endeavor.

The truth is, we can't change others. We can't control their actions or beliefs. What we can control is our response and how we choose to allocate our energy. It's essential to recognize that the need to be right or prove a point can consume significant mental and emotional resources.

By releasing the burden of trying to change someone else, we free ourselves from mental torment and emotional exhaustion. We conserve our energy for more productive and fulfilling pursuits, allowing us to focus on personal growth and inner peace.

Today, I remind myself to save energy and let go of the need to change others. Instead, I choose to invest in my well-being and growth.

**Meditative Reflection "Word of the Day"**

## MY JOURNAL ENTRY

## October 20, 2022

## Word of the Day: "Silence"

Breathe in. Breathe Out.

Today, during my meditation, the word silence floated into my space.

Silence is an energy. Silence helps me quiet the inner chatter. Silence helps me hear my soul. Silence is my safe space. Silence is a remedy for internal growth. Silence is my guidance. Silence allows time for reflection. Silence is a positive energy I crave. My creativity is found in silence. Self-forgiveness is forged during my silent, grace-filled meditation. Silence shields out the noise and opinions of others.

Silence is a resource.

## Deeper Connection Within

1. What do you need to tell yourself the truth about?

_____

_____

_____

_____

_____

_____

2. What immediate action can you take to reduce stress and anxiety?

_____

_____

_____

_____

_____

3. What decisions do you need to make to create peace in your life?

_____

_____

_____

_____

_____

_____

**Gratitude Reflection of the Day**

I'm thankful for the inner strength that guides me to love and appreciate myself more with each passing day.

It's <u>One Year</u> from now.

Write a letter to yourself titled "Moved On." What happened when you stopped allowing negative thoughts and people to control your life?

_____

_____

_____

_____

_____

_____

_____

_____

_____

_____

_____

_____

_____

_____

_____

_____

_____

_____

_____

_____

_____

_____

_____

DAY 9

# Dig Up Pain

## Forgiveness Thought of the Day

Today's Forgiveness Thought of the Day invites us to confront the pain we've buried deep within, urging us to dig it up and face our struggles. It's a profound reflection that resonates with my journey of self-discovery and healing.

Throughout our lives, we all encounter obstacles and setbacks, some so substantial that they can leave us overwhelmed and tempted to give up. It's a natural response to avoid pain and discomfort, smother our struggles, and hide from our fears.

But what if we practiced working through it instead of being paralyzed by fear? What if we embraced the challenges as opportunities for growth and transformation? This thought reminds us that we have the strength and resilience to face our pain head-on.

Acknowledging our struggles and digging up the buried pain, we begin a profound journey of self-discovery and healing. It's a courageous step toward personal growth and empowerment. It's an act of self-compassion and self-love.

Today, I embrace working through my fears and confronting my struggles. I choose to dig up the pain and use it as a catalyst for growth and transformation. I recognize that the potential for profound healing and empowerment lies within these challenges.

**Meditative Reflection "Word of the Day"**

## MY JOURNAL ENTRY

### September 28, 2022

### Word of the Day: "Open"

Breathe in. Breathe out. Open.

Today's word, which flowed to me, was open.

Open-minded thoughts bring prosperity. Open hands receive. Open to God's correction. Openness to wisdom takes me to new places.

Open to serendipitous miracles. Openness to help is wisdom. Being open to asking for what I want is my belief in the worthiness of my desire. Being open to learning is a gift to grow. Being open to healing leads to growth. Open to welcoming my inner zeal.

Open to expressing words of inspiration as I look in the mirror. Open to change is maturity. Open to walk away is surrender. Being open to rebuilding is strength.

Open to restore is faith. Being open to push through is belief in the impossible. Open to adventure is playfulness. Openness takes me to the highest frequency of life, passion, and connection.

If I am open to receive, listen, grow, learn, love, surrender, give, ask, heal, forgive, move on, and let go, my life will be abundantly blessed.

**Deeper Connection Within:**

1. What must you forgive yourself for?

2. What are you afraid of letting go of and why?

3. I forgive myself, and I am open to receive _____

_____

_____

_____ as I nurse my wounds.

**Gratitude Reflection of the Day**

Today, I am filled with gratitude for the resilience of my spirit, which allows me to bounce back from challenges and setbacks.

**Forgiveness Exercise of the Day:**

Write a letter to yourself about the pain you dug up and what you replanted to thrive and grow.

_____

_____

_____

_____

_____

_____

_____

_____

_____

_____

_____

_____

_____

_____

_____

_____

_____

_____

_____

_____

_____

_____

_____

# Apologies Don't Heal Pain

## Forgiveness Thought of the Day

Today's Forgiveness Thought of the Day is a poignant reminder that apologies, while important, don't automatically mend the pain. This reflection deeply resonates with my own experiences and insights.

I've noticed how we often assign great significance to receiving apologies, almost as if they possess a magical power to heal the wounds caused by someone's actions. Yet, in reality, apologies alone can't guarantee genuine healing. Sometimes, they can mask empty words and manipulation without sincere remorse.

I've been in situations where I apologized without genuinely altering my behavior. At times, I did it to move forward or repair a relationship, clinging to the hope that my apology would erase the stain of my actions. More often than not, this hope remained unfulfilled.

Interestingly, we frequently hold others accountable for their actions and insist on their growth and change, but we may not always afford ourselves and others the same compassion. We might find ourselves waiting for an apology from someone else before we feel justified in embarking on our healing journey.

However, it's crucial to ponder: What if that awaited apology never arrives? Why should someone else's reluctance to say "I'm sorry" hinder our growth and healing? We must recognize that our healing journey ultimately rests in our own hands, irrespective of whether we receive an apology from external sources.

**Meditative Reflection "Word of the Day"**

## MY JOURNAL ENTRY

### September 16, 2022

**Word of the Day "Wholeness"**

Breathe in. Breathe out. Wholeness.

Today, during my meditation, the word wholeness connected with me.

Wholeness means complete. Wholeness, after a relationship ends, understands the memories will last a lifetime, and some parts of me may be bruised, but I am still whole.

Wholeness knows I did my best despite still having unanswered questions. Wholeness also realizes I don't need all the answers to move on. Wholeness is accepting even if I know all the answers; things may still be the same.

Wholeness is looking inward for the answers because no one else can complete me. Wholeness knows when "it" is complete. Wholeness knows it's safe to let go and move on.

Wholeness is regulating my nervous system by breathing in and breathing out. Wholeness is accepting myself just as I am. Wholeness means no longer seeking validation.

Wholeness is healing without an apology. Wholeness is walking away when it no longer serves me. Wholeness is listening to my inner child whispering, "I am safe."

Wholeness is sharing my story with only some. Wholeness is finding peace with being misunderstood. Wholeness is saying "no" without an explanation. Wholeness is being happy about not receiving the invitation. Wholeness is no longer trying to understand why.

Wholeness is releasing the hurt while learning the lesson. Although wholeness shifts from day to day, I am always complete. Wholeness is accepting all parts of me.

Wholeness releases me from the false illusion others will save me. Wholeness is internal accountability. Wholeness is taking responsibility.

Wholeness is my solo journey while sometimes traveling alongside others. Wholeness is my footsteps in the sand.

Wholeness is holding my hand. Wholeness is creating joyfulness in the silence. Wholeness is accepting it.

Wholeness is closing the door to the memories keeping me stagnant.

Wholeness is making a comeback. Wholeness is forgiveness. Wholeness is welcoming newness. Wholeness is all of my experiences, habits, and beliefs blended, creating a healthier me.

I am whole even when they walk away. I am whole when I'm alone. I am whole when I feel disconnected. I am whole during the storm. I am whole when I'm the only one celebrating.

I'm whole when money isn't flowing. I'm whole when money is abundant. I'm whole when no one understands. I'm whole when I want to be alone. I am whole when people put me down. I am whole when people disconnect.

Nothing needs to be added or subtracted. I am always whole and complete.

## Deeper Connection Within

1. What does wholeness mean to me?

_____

_____

_____

_____

2. What memories cause me not to feel whole?

_____

_____

_____

_____

3. I have the power to_____

_____

even if _____
_____ never apologies to me for
_____.

## Gratitude Reflection of the Day

I'm grateful for the moments of self-reflection and self-discovery that led me to greater self-appreciation.

**Forgiveness Exercise of the Day:**

Write a letter to yourself about how redefining wholeness transformed your life.

I Am Thriving in my inner peace.

_____
_____
_____
_____
_____
_____
_____
_____
_____
_____
_____
_____
_____
_____
_____
_____
_____
_____
_____
_____
_____

# Your Emotions Matter

## Peace of Mind

### Forgiveness Thought of the Day

In life, I realize that I spend more time dwelling on my dislikes and fears than on my dreams and aspirations. My thoughts are powerful energy carriers, and what I focus on tends to manifest in my life. So, when was the last time I intentionally directed my thoughts towards positivity? Imagine if I celebrated the inherent greatness within me, gazing into the mirror with appreciation for my smile, laughter, personality, and choices.

This shift in focus toward my inner beauty opens doors for self-acceptance and helps me see the beauty in others. As I embarked on my journey of self-forgiveness, allowing myself to learn and grow from my mistakes rather than harshly judging them taught me patience and kindness towards others.

It dawned on me that the judgments or labels I place on others are often a reflection of my self-perceptions. It's a reminder that the way I view others mirrors my inner world.

Positive shifts in mindset are like ripples in a pond, touching every facet of my life. Embracing positivity begins with acknowledging the greatness within, extending to how I perceive and interact with the world around me.

**Meditative Reflection "Word of the Day"**

**MY JOURNAL ENTRY**

**September 12, 2022**

**Word of the Day "Belief"**

Breathe in. Breathe out Belief.

It all comes together when I believe. Believe I am valuable. Believe it will happen to me. Believe it when I can't see it. Believe when doubt creeps in. Believe magic will always happen. Believe God wants the best for me. Believe when it's scary.

Believe when everyone walks away. Believe when all hope is lost.

Believing is faith. Belief leaves space for miracles. Belief makes room for manifestations. Self-belief boosts confidence. Build self-belief as strong as the roots of a 100-year-old oak tree.

Believe the "impossible" is always possible. Believe people will show up. I believe God will keep his promises to me. Believe people want to help. Believe it will work out. Believe I deserve more. Believe good things happen to people like me. Believe it will get better.

Believe when one else does. Believe when people walk away. Believe when it feels impossible. Believe in moments of uncertainty. Belief requires trust. Belief is the icing on faith's cake.

Belief is faith in action. Believe in serendipitous outcomes. Believe in magic. Believe my intuition. Believe in favor. Believe a grateful heart makes dreams come true.

**Deeper Connection Within:**

1. I forgive myself, and I am ready, to be honest with myself about _____
_____
_____.

2. I forgive myself, and I am ready to tell _____
_____
_____the truth about
_____
_____.

3. I forgive myself and will no longer water myself down to please _____
_____
_____.

**Gratitude Reflection of the Day**

I appreciate the joy that comes from embracing and loving myself fully, realizing that it radiates outward and touches those around me.

**Forgiveness Exercise of the Day:**

It's <u>One Year</u> Later.

Write a letter about how your belief in yourself boosted your confidence and transformed your life.

_____

_____

_____

_____

_____

_____

_____

_____

_____

_____

_____

_____

_____

_____

_____

_____

_____

_____

_____

_____

_____

# Healing Takes Time
# Shield Out Drama

## Forgiveness Thought of the Day

Have I ever found myself in a situation where I believed I had all the facts, only to realize later that my conclusions were based on incomplete or entirely false information? Oh yes, I've been there. I mentally rehearsed how I would confront someone, ready with my well-prepared arguments and unwilling to back down. Even when I eventually discovered the truth, my pride and ego often pushed me to proceed with the confrontation, unwilling to humble myself.

It's intriguing how many of us claim to dislike drama, yet our thoughts, actions, reactions, and behaviors frequently invite it into our lives. How can I expect positive outcomes when I habitually rehearse worst-case scenarios? How often do I meditate on things working out in my favor?

Shielding myself from drama begins with my self-talk and extends to my conversations with others. I'm committed to eliminating gossip, negative talk, and toxic communication from my interactions. I've come to recognize that our conversations profoundly impact our lives, shaping our experiences and outcomes.

So, today, I focus on positive interactions, and nurturing conversations that uplift and inspire. I understand that by shielding out drama, I pave the way for more harmonious and fulfilling connections with others.

Also, if the information pertains to me, proceed with probing

questions versus the attack strategy.

**Meditative Reflection "Word of the Day"**

**MY JOURNAL ENTRY**

**September 8, 2022**

**Word of the Day "Healing"**

Breathe In. Breathe Out.

Healing the false identity I created. Healing my urge to receive the approval of others. Healing my need to be right all the time. Healing my money wounds. Healing my relationship with food. Healing my communication habits.

I am healing my desire to control others. I am healing my unconscious connection to low-grade miracles. I am healing my negative thoughts. I am healing my soul. Healing my manipulative habits, conscious or subconscious. I am healing my lack of accountability.

I am healing my unfocused parts. Healing the lies, I tell myself. I am healing my attachment to perfectionism and my desire always to be understood. I am healing my inner child. I am healing my emotional wounds. I am healing my invisible scars. I am healing my traumatic memories. I am healing my attachments to actions I regret. I am healing my desire to be liked by most. I am healing my passion for controlling my children's lives.

I am healing my self-imposed pressure. I am healing my unhealthy connection with others. I am healing my attachments to trusting others more than I trust myself. I am healing the emotional scars I wear for others. I am healing from not showing up for me. I am healing from shrinking to fit in. I am healing from the decisions I regret.

Healing from emotions, I didn't express. Healing from friendships I destroyed, relationships I bruised, and not forgiving myself. I am healing from forgiving others more than I forgave myself. I am healing from my unmet expectations. I am healing from blaming others instead of being accountable. I am healing from misunderstandings.

I am healing from unresolved anger, known or unknown. I am healing from self-imposed pressure. I am healing from feelings of abandonment. I am healing from speaking when silence was the cure. I am healing from being a bully. I am healing from being bullied. I am healing from negative self-talk. I was healing from limiting beliefs.

Healing from holding back tears. Healing from not fully connecting within. Healing my emotional regret. Healing my lack of patience.

Healing is my decision. Healing is a gift I choose to give myself over and over and over again. Healing is the connection to my soul. Healing gives me the confidence to move on. Healing brings me hope. Healing is the pen to write my story.

Healing is what my soul yearns for. Healing is always ready to protect, teach, and nurture me. Healing transforms everything. Healing patiently waits for an invitation in.

Healing is a guardian angel, always ready to guide me through the rough patches.

Thank you for my healing. Thank you for my healing. Thank you for my healing.

## Deeper Connection Within

1. Who or what must I release to become your dream person?

_____

_____

_____

_____

_____

2. What wounds are unhealed and why?

_____

_____

_____

_____

_____

3. How can I build trust with myself?

_____

_____

_____

_____

_____

## Gratitude Reflection of the Day

Today, I send loving energy to my heart, nurturing the love and appreciation I have for myself.

**Forgiveness Exercise of the Day:**

Write a letter to yourself about your healthy habits to shield out drama.

_____
_____
_____
_____
_____
_____
_____
_____
_____
_____
_____
_____
_____
_____
_____
_____
_____
_____
_____
_____
_____
_____

# Resentment Equals Clinging

## Overcoming Anxiety & Stress

### Forgiveness Thought of the Day

In my journey of self-forgiveness and healing, I've come to understand the importance of identifying and managing my emotional triggers, especially when it comes to dealing with anxiety and stress.

The first step is always acknowledgment. I must recognize what is causing me discomfort and be honest about it. No one else can define my feelings for me; it's a deeply personal process.

I've learned that stressful events are a part of life, and moments of self-doubt are inevitable. But instead of seeking external validation for how I should feel, I've created a support system. This system covers my mental and emotional well-being and physical health, as these aspects are closely interconnected.

I've empowered myself to better understand my triggers through curiosity and vulnerability. This self-awareness has allowed me to respond more skillfully to challenging situations. It's a continuous journey, but I'm building resilience and finding greater peace within myself with each step.

## Deeper Connection Within

1. What does a clear release from stress mean to me?

_____

_____

_____

_____

_____

2. What childhood wounds are still tender and why?

_____

_____

_____

_____

_____

3. I am ready to trust myself by _____

_____

_____

_____.

## Gratitude Reflection of the Day

I'm thankful for the transformative power of self-forgiveness, which frees me from the shackles of regret and self-criticism.

# Meditative Reflection "Word of the Day"

## MY JOURNAL ENTRY

## September 14, 2022

## Words of the Day "Clear Release"

Breathe in. Breathe out.

I am releasing my attachment to outcomes. Clear release of inner connections to things holding me back. Clear release of attachments that no longer serve me. Clear release of links to "how it" will happen. Clear release from limiting thoughts.

Clear release from inner agreements minimizing me.

Clear release from low-level energy. My clear release makes room for more of what I want. Clear release disconnects my limitations. Clear release cuts ties.

Clear release builds bridges to connect with what I want. Clear release disconnects memories from the constant loop of agony. A clear release is the sound of silence.

My clear release is stillness. My clear release is vulnerability. My clear release is that the path ahead will sustain me and release my faith. My clear release is unity within.

A clear release is trusting myself.

A clear release is a conscious decision. A clear release is letting go of what is holding me back. My clear release is a solo journey of self-discovery.

My clear release allows me to welcome the highest vibration of blissfulness.

**Forgiveness Exercise of the Day:**

For the next 24 hours, journal your:

Daily sleep regimen. Log your food intake.

Write down your exercise routine (if you have one).

In the evenings, reflect on your mood for the day.

What brought you the most joy? What were your primary thoughts?

_____

_____

_____

_____

_____

_____

_____

_____

_____

_____

_____

_____

_____

# Realistic Expectations

## Forgiveness Thought of the Day

As I reflect on my own self-imposed expectations, I can't help but realize how they have influenced my relationships, sometimes in ways I didn't intend. Wanting the best for someone can inadvertently come across as judgment, which has strained some of my closest connections. I've heard loved ones express feelings of pressure, and their words, "Nothing is ever good enough for you," struck a chord.

It's become clear that I often hold expectations for others that I don't apply to myself. When someone I care about criticizes me, I hope for an apology. But I must ask myself, when was the last time I apologized to myself for the negative self-talk? When did I last look in the mirror and say, "I forgive you"?

It's a common pattern; many of us engage in relentless negative self-talk when we make mistakes. We expect understanding and forgiveness from others, but we often neglect to offer the same compassion to ourselves. This reflection reminds me of the importance of self-compassion and how it can positively impact my relationship with myself and my interactions with those I love.

The most realistic expectation is smothering yourself with the love you crave from others.

My realistic expectation is to forgive myself first.

My realistic expectation is to be kind to myself.

My realistic expectation is to set boundaries and enforce them.

My realistic expectation is positive self-talk.

My realistic expectation is to walk away from unhealthy relationships, even if they are family.

My realistic expectation is to be treated with kindness.

My realistic expectation is for people to appreciate me.

My realistic expectation is for me to accomplish my goals before helping others.

My realistic expectation is to ask for what I want.

# Meditative Reflection "Word of the Day"
## MY JOURNAL ENTRY
### October 1, 2022
### Word of the Day "Dep"

Breathe in. Breathe out.

Today, during my meditation, the letter "DEP" floated into my space. I immediately looked for positive words as I tried to figure out what word it could be.

Then God reminded me, *"Not every "positive" word or "negative" word is as it appears.*

Dig deeper into meanings to discover what I am trying to teach you and where I intend to take you."

Then the word deprive floated in clearly. I kept thinking this couldn't be it cause it meant something was taken from me. "Will I lose something?"

Then God told me again,

*"Is every action you take serving you? Don't you need to deprive yourself of certain things to get where you are going? Why do you need access to everything to get what you want?*

*Deprivation can be good. Deprivation from television will minimize distractions. Deprivations from social media will limit jealousy and comparison.*

*Deprivation from friends who gossip will minimize your judgment of others. Deprivation from a busy social calendar will give more time for what matters. Deprivation from negative thoughts gives space for restoration. Deprivation from limited behaviors brings playfulness.*

*So what are you willing to deprive yourself of to live? Deprivation of your comfort brings lasting results. Deprivation from excessive sugar adds decades to your life. It's time for you to make clear, intentional decisions about what you will deprive yourself of to access the life you pray for and dream of. It's all waiting for you. Walk into it."*

## Deeper Connection Within

1. What are some unrealistic expectations I have for myself and others? List them.

_____

_____

_____

_____

_____

2. My unrealistic expectations towards _____

_____

have caused me to judge them as_____

___, and today, I welcome new thoughts to support my healing journey.

3. I forgive _____

_____ for

_____

_____

_____and release my attachment to

_____

_____

_____.

## Gratitude Reflection of the Day

I appreciate the confidence that arises as I acknowledge my strengths and talents, bolstering my belief in myself.

**Forgiveness Exercise of the Day:**

It's <u>One Year</u> from now.

Write a letter about how depriving yourself of something or someone transformed your life.

---

 

 

 

 

 

 

 

 

 

 

 

 

 

 

 

 

 

 

 

 

 

 

*PART III*

# GROW

## Welcome Inner Peace

# Commit to the Journey

## Forgiveness Thought of the Day

Questions swirled relentlessly in my mind, each one laden with guilt and self-reflection. "Why am I easily irritated by minor, insignificant things?" "Why does my temper flare when my children make innocent mistakes?" "Why am I often impatient with my husband?"

Initiating my journey toward inner peace and self-forgiveness, I took a significant step. I asked my family to be my mirrors, to "call me out" when they noticed my obnoxious behavior and unreasonable reactions. It was a commitment I made to uncover my core issues and identify the stress triggers that sent me spiraling.

Their accountability became an unexpected gift, helping me navigate the complexities of my emotions. My family embraced the opportunity to point out my shortcomings lovingly, and I welcomed their input with open arms. It was an acknowledgment of my willingness to grow and evolve.

This process taught me that self-awareness and a commitment to change are vital aspects of the forgiveness journey. It's not just about forgiving others but also about forgiving ourselves and actively working on becoming better versions of ourselves. The support of loved ones on this path has been an invaluable asset, and together, we've taken steps toward greater understanding, compassion, and inner peace.

### Meditative Reflection "Word of the Day"

## MY JOURNAL ENTRY

## September 3, 2022

## Words of the Day "Walk In"

Breathe In...Breathe Out

Surrender to overflow. I expect a massive influx of wealth to flow continuously to me. I have found my path. I have embraced my journey.

Walk in abundance. Walk in expectation. Walk in the light. Walk into a surrendered space. Walk in with the acceptance of overflow. Walk in playfully. Walk in confident.

Walk in openness. Walk in connected to my truth. Walk in with authority. Walk in expectancy. Walk in courageously. Walk in euphoric, Walk in fiercely. Walk in boldly.

Walk in as I belong. Walk in understanding. Walk in, creating space. Walk in, making space. Walk in aligned. Walk in, asking questions. Walk in fun-loving. Walk in quickly.

Walk in freely. Walk in calmly. Walk in unsure. Walk in passionately. Walk in needing more confidence. Walk in brilliantly. Walk in smart. Walk in head high. Walk in alone. Walk in determined. Walk in with an expectation. Walk in delighted. Walk in for solutions. Walk in bravely. Walk in to listen. Walk in to learn. Walk in to grow. Walk in to be a healer. Walk in for mentorship. Walk in to mentor. Walk in with genius ideas. Walk in to build. Walk in to reconnect. Walk in to restore.

Walk in to rejuvenate me. Walk in to renew. Walk in to reclaim. Walk in to rebuild. Walk in to protect. Walk in and speak up. Walk in and be still. Walk in silence.

Walk in to create my destiny. Walk in and dream. Walk into my journey. Walk towards my future. Walk through my struggles. Walk past the failures.

Walk into the life I desire. Walk through the rain. Walk through the depression. Walk with positive thoughts. Walk while building inner strength. Walk to keep moving forward.

Walk into who I am becoming. Walk when I am tired. Walk fearfully. Walk in encouragement. Walk in love. Walk with my light. Walk in integrity. Walk in unity.

Walk and create my path. Walk in creativity. Walk in harmony. Walk to the beat of my drum. Walk fulfilled. Walk feeling empty. Walk without explaining. Walk in triumphant.

Walk and talk to God. Walk and listen to God. Walk and connect with people. Walk and meet new friends. Walk and unite with my inner soul. Walk and align with my vision.

Walk into my passion and purpose. Walk and build inner trust. Walk and listen to my heart. Walk in forgiveness. Walk in your anointing. Walk in growth. Walk in wholeheartedness. Walk in patience. Walk and welcome help. Walk and ask for help. Walk and ask for forgiveness. Walk in self-acceptance. Walk in kindness.

Walk in belief in others. Walk in expectation of good. Walk in mesmerized. Walk forward expecting miracles. Walk in clarity. Walk with positive thoughts for others.

Walk with belief in myself. Walk in self-forgiveness. Walk in healing money wounds. Walk in, honoring my boundaries. Walk in acceptance of massive wealth.

Walk in expectation of excellent health. Walk in, forgiving my body. Walk in the forgiveness of my past. Walk in forgiveness towards those who didn't handle me with care in the past. Walk in expectation of greatness.

Walk in knowing people love me. Walk in knowing I am lovable. Walk in knowing I am always forgivable.

Walk in knowing they may never understand. Walk in accepting my truth. Walk in the fullness of me. I will walk into my legacy.

Upon reflection on my writing on this day, I realized I had written numerous ways to walk in to accept and receive abundance in every area.

## Deeper Connection Within

Imagine five years have passed. You have yet to make _minimal_ progress toward your dreams. Write a letter to your future self five years from now describing what's happening in your life.

_____

_____

_____

_____

_____

_____

_____

_____

Imagine five years have passed. You are _disciplined and have committed_ to your dreams. Write a letter to your future self five years from now describing what's happening in your life.

_____

_____

_____

_____

_____

_____

_____

_____

## Gratitude Reflection of the Day

I'm grateful for the moments when I choose self-love over self-doubt, recognizing that it leads to greater happiness and fulfillment.

**Forgiveness Exercise of the Day:**

Journal about your thoughts and emotions after the "5 Years Into The Future" letters.

_____

_____

_____

_____

_____

_____

_____

_____

_____

_____

_____

_____

_____

_____

_____

_____

_____

_____

_____

_____

_____

_____

_____

_____

# Plant & Water Healing

## Forgiveness Thought of the Day

Often, I find myself listening to people as they "vent" about their lives, explaining why they feel stuck. It seems to revolve around what others have done to them, how they perceive a lack of support, or how they shoulder the blame for every failure and fear they face. It's genuinely heart-wrenching to witness how people can verbally abuse and diminish themselves, seemingly oblivious to how their words shape their present reality.

One fundamental truth I've come to understand is that the energy we exude through our words, thoughts, and actions acts like a magnet, drawing similar energies back into our lives. It begs the question: How can one expect to establish healthy boundaries, nurture positive self-talk, or cultivate a loving family dynamic when their focus remains fixated on past trauma, ongoing struggle, and discord?

This realization has led me to recognize the profound importance of planting seeds of healing, positivity, and self-compassion in my life. As a gardener tends to their plants, I must nurture these seeds with love, care, and intention. Watering them daily with affirmations, self-forgiveness, and gratitude, I create an environment that fosters growth within myself and the world around me.

So, remember that we are the gardeners of our lives. By planting seeds of healing and watering them with positivity, we can transform our inner landscapes and manifest a reality filled with love, abundance, and inner peace.

**Meditative Reflection "Word of the Day"**

## MY JOURNAL ENTRY

## October 6, 2022

### Word of the Day "Enlarge."

Breathe in. Breathe out.

Today, as I meditated, the word enlarge floated into my space.

Enlarge my faith. Enlarge my thoughtfulness. Enlarge my container for money. Enlarge my inner peace. Enlarge my friendship connections. Enlarge my bandwidth to receive.

Enlarge my belief in people. Enlarge my faith within. Enlarge my compassion. Enlarge my vortex for wealth. Enlarge my creative genius. Enlarge my ability to transform lives.

Enlarge my impact on society to forgive themselves first. Enlarge my reach to spread warmhearted messages. Enlarge my protection. Enlarge my belief in my children.

Enlarge the passion in my marriage. Enlarge my creative genius. Enlarge my legacy. Enlarge my resources. Enlarge my vision for the future. Enlarge my reach.

Enlarge my bank accounts. Enlarge my assets and portfolio. Enlarge my global empire. Enlarge the change I bring to others. Enlarge my voice. Enlarge my positive presence.

Enlarge my inner unity. Enlarge my belief in ease and flow. Enlarge my connections. Enlarge my relationships with people. Enlarge divine my connections.

Enlarge manifestations in my life. Enlarge my good encounters. Enlarge me. Enlarge my faith. Enlarge me. Enlarge my ability to be still. Enlarge my unity within. Enlarge my faith in God.

Enlarge my intuitions. Enlarge my healing power. Enlarge my capacity to connect to source energy. Enlarge my understanding.

Enlarge my enlightenment. Enlarge my lightheartedness. Enlarge my hope in humanity. Enlarge my reach to touch others. Enlarge my space to support families with mending generational wounds. Enlarge my ability to silence the noise.

Enlarge my mind, body, and soul.

## Deeper Connection Within

1. What would happen if I let go of the emotional baggage?

_____

_____

_____

_____

_____

2. I accept _____

_____happened, and I will no longer allow it to mean

_____

_____ about me.

3. My new boundary is _____

_____

_____, and I am capable of speaking up to protect it.

## Gratitude Reflection of the Day

Today, I am grateful for the beauty of my unique journey and the lessons it has taught me.

**Forgiveness Exercise of the Day:**

It's <u>One Year</u> from now.

What "enlarged" in your life since you planted healing?

_____

_____

_____

_____

_____

_____

_____

_____

_____

_____

_____

_____

_____

_____

_____

_____

_____

_____

_____

_____

_____

_____

_____

_____

# Give Grace

## Forgiveness Thought of the Day

Surrendering to my needs is an act of self-compassion, and it's something I've learned to embrace on my journey of self-forgiveness. It involves being gentle with myself and acknowledging my limits and vulnerabilities.

It's all too easy to push myself relentlessly, demanding perfection and unwavering strength. However, this only leads to burnout and inner turmoil.

One powerful tool I've found on this path is mindfulness. Mindfulness and meditation allow us to enter a state of alert and focused relaxation. They encourage me to pay deliberate and non-judgmental attention to my thoughts and sensations. It's a practice that contradicts my natural inclination to constantly judge, question, and analyze.

Through mindfulness, I've learned to be present with my emotions and to acknowledge them without criticism or judgment. It's a space where I can extend grace to myself, recognizing that I am human with my own set of needs and limitations. Surrendering to these needs has brought a profound sense of inner peace and self-acceptance.

So, as I navigate my forgiveness journey, let me remember the power of giving myself grace and the transformative practice of mindfulness. In these moments of surrender, I discover the strength that comes from self-compassion and the ability to navigate life's challenges with greater resilience and inner peace.

**Deeper Connection Within:**

1. What does surrender mean to me?

_____

_____

_____

_____

_____

2. How can I give myself grace?

_____

_____

_____

_____

_____

3. What can you do to create better connections within?

_____

_____

_____

_____

_____

**Gratitude Reflection of the Day**

I'm thankful for the inner peace that comes when I forgive myself and fully embrace the love I have for myself.

# Meditative Reflection "Word of the Day"

## MY JOURNAL ENTRY

## September 4, 2022

## Word of the Day "Surrender"

Surrender to pleasure. Surrender to peace. Surrender to my life transforming.

Surrender to the emotional rehabilitation process. Surrender to the journey.

Surrender to my commitment. Surrender to my inner truth. Surrender to love.

Surrender to my life. Surrender to God's will.

Surrender to my intuition. Surrender as a mother.

Surrendering strengthens my faith.

## Deeper Connection Within

I surrender to _____
_____ and accept vulnerability and self-honesty is a
_____
_____ in my self-love journey.
I surrender to having _____
_____ in my life.
I can vocalize what I want and still be _____
_____.

## Gratitude Reflection of the Day

I am grateful for the wisdom and strength to surrender
and trust everything is working in my favor.

## Forgiveness Exercises of the Day:

Write a letter to yourself about gently surrendering to your emotional needs.

_____

_____

_____

_____

_____

_____

_____

_____

_____

_____

_____

_____

_____

_____

_____

_____

_____

_____

_____

_____

_____

_____

# Create New Habits

## Forgiveness Thought of the Day

Creating new habits has been a crucial part of my journey towards forgiving myself first. It's a process that requires self-compassion, patience, and a willingness to change. When we acknowledge our past mistakes and decide to embark on a path of self-forgiveness, we often realize that old habits and thought patterns no longer serve us.

The key to success is creating new, healthier habits aligning with our healing journey. This can encompass various aspects of our lives, from talking to ourselves to how we treat our bodies and interact with others.

One of the most impactful habits has been practicing self-compassion in my self-talk. I've learned to replace self-criticism with words of kindness and understanding. This shift in my internal dialogue has been transformative, helping me release the weight of guilt and shame.

Another important habit has been setting boundaries to protect my emotional well-being. I've learned to say no when necessary and prioritize self-care, recognizing that taking care of myself is not selfish but essential for healing.

Creating these new habits has been difficult, and I've had my share of setbacks. However, the key is not perfection but persistence. Each day is an opportunity to reinforce these positive habits; over time, they have become a natural part of my life.

So, as you embark on your forgiveness journey, remember that creating new habits is a powerful way to support and reinforce your commitment to self-forgiveness and self-compassion. It's a journey of growth and transformation; every step forward is a victory.

**Meditative Reflection "Word of the Day"**

**MY JOURNAL ENTRY**

**October 29, 2022**

**Word of the Day "Normalize"**

Breathe in. Breathe out.

Today, during my meditation, the word normalize floated into my space.

I began thinking about mother/daughter relations and how so many women find comfort in their retaliatory actions towards their mothers. "She neglected me." "She wasn't good enough." "She didn't do enough." "I am just giving her back what she gave me."

Telling themselves it is warranted to be rude, short, agitated, frustrated, or annoyed during most conversations or dismissive.

I am committed to normalizing being tender towards my mother when I speak to her.

Blessings flowed differently when I became compassionate when I spoke about my mom. I was caring in my thoughts towards her.

I became mindful about repairing my childhood and adult wounds.

I normalized valuing my mother while she was alive to avoid living with remorse when she died.

Normalize being patient, friendly, and appreciative towards my mother.

Healing was a gift. I realized if I spoke to an employer the way I talked to my loved ones, I would be fired."

I stopped minimizing my behavior as "I'm always misunderstood" and became accountable. I normalized changing my behavior as the best form of apology.

I normalized speaking nicely. I normalized being cheerful. I normalized telling the truth even if it cost me something. I normalized forgiving myself before forgiving others.

I normalized saying no. I have normalized walking away when it no longer feeds my soul. Normalize saying yes to people, places, or things delightful in my life even if no one else understands.

Normalize having fun. Normalize being playful. Normalize thinking out of the box. Normalize seeing the good.

Normalize listening more than I speak. Normalize asking questions first. Normalize being silent. Normalize speaking up. Normalize doing my inner work without guilting others.

Normalize expecting healthy outcomes. Normalize taking action. Normalize asking for help. Normalize going solo. Normalize believing in myself more than others.

Normalize counting on me. Normalize making myself proud. Normalize eating healthy. Normalize being wealthy. Normalize receiving kind words. Normalize resting.

Normalize relaxing my mind, body, and soul. Normalize patience. Normalize things flowing with ease. Normalize forgiving myself. Normalize forgiving others.

Normalize healing my money wounds. Normalize smiling at people genuinely.

Normalize being grateful for paying bills. Normalize self-appreciation.

Normalize genuinely celebrating others. Normalize giving with no strings attached. Normalize showing up for myself. Normalize giving myself grace. Normalize, giving myself space to grow. Normalize asking for what I want. Normalize changing my mind without feeling guilty. Normalize admiring myself.

Normalize apologizing. Normalize being thoughtful to myself. Normalize seeing the good in all situations. Normalize taking the advice I give.

Normalize taking responsibility for my life without blaming others. Normalize being accountable for my actions. Normalize speaking positively of people even when they're in a rough patch.

Normalize keeping people's information confidential. Normalize keeping my word. Normalize shining my light. Normalize charging for my services.

Normalize raising my prices with confidence. Normalize valuing my reflection in the mirror. Normalize being vulnerable with myself.

## Deeper Connection Within

I am worthy of having my needs met and still be ____
_____.

I permit myself to be open to receiving help and still
be _____.

I give myself permission to show up as my whole self
and still be _____
_____.

## Gratitude Reflection of the Day

I appreciate the moments of clarity and self-acceptance
that allow me to let go of negative self-perceptions.

**Forgiveness Exercises of the Day:**

It's <u>One Year</u> from now.

Write a letter about what you normalized in your life and how it transformed your relationships.

_____

_____

_____

_____

_____

_____

_____

_____

_____

_____

_____

_____

_____

_____

_____

_____

_____

_____

_____

_____

_____

_____

_____

# Memories (Re-Write Your Story)

## Forgiveness Thought of the Day

I want to emphasize that recognizing how our past experiences have shaped our present selves should never be mistaken as an acceptance that we deserved any harm or wrongdoing. It's essential to remember that we cannot alter the past, and the pain we carry is not a reflection of our worthiness. This realization is at the core of our journey towards self-forgiveness.

For me personally, grasping this truth marked a turning point in my life. I came to understand that while I couldn't change the past, I held the power to reshape how I perceived it and how it influenced my future. It was within the scars of my life, those indelible marks left by past experiences, that I unearthed the strength to become the person I was destined to be.

My own journey through these scars led me to establish the Forgiveness Lifestyle Movement, a global community dedicated to healing and embracing self-forgiveness. These scars transformed into a wellspring of resilience and empowerment.

When we allow our past to dictate our future, we become trapped in a cycle of pain and resentment. However, the moment we make the choice to rewrite our story, we reclaim our power. The trauma and those who inflicted it no longer hold sway over our thoughts and actions. We step into our own authority, crafting a future not dictated by our past but illuminated by our newfound strength and self-forgiveness.

# Example of My Story from a Victim Mindset:

While other high school graduates were preparing for college, I was picking out a baby stroller.

I became pregnant with my beautiful daughter a few months after my high school graduation.

Then, eight and a half months after she was born, my handsome son arrived.

So, by the age of 19, I was the mother of two infants.

Their father's involvement was sparingly and almost nonexistent when they were toddlers.

He had a child with another woman four months after my son was born.

Being a single teenage mother with two children felt unbearable at times.

I was paying rent, car payments, insurance, utilities, groceries, and expenses for the children with no child support.

Teenage parenthood left me feeling lonely, isolated, abandoned, and rejected by society.

# Example of My Story from Victorious Mindset

Even though society deemed me another young, incompetent teen mom doomed to be on welfare forever, I chose to see the light.

Though it was dim, it was light; for me, it meant hope.

Perseverance, determination, and relentlessness propelled me to excel for my babies.

With the advice and guidance of my mother, I got a job at a law firm.

I went to college at night and worked a 9 to 5, struggling to push through.

The attorneys and paralegals convinced me to purchase my first home at 24 years old.

Although it was challenging God's grace and my earth angels were my guiding lights.

Being a single mother taught me independence, drive, and how to dream big and create magic with very little.

Do you see the difference in the stories?

One story comes from a place of helplessness, and the other from a place of power.

Everyone has experienced discomfort, trauma, and suffering. Identifying your emotional triggers and taking action to shift your narrative allows you to use your past experiences as a stepping stone and not a roadblock.

You are a beautiful gift and a light in the world, regardless of whether others acknowledge it. Own your beauty.

Embrace all of your beautiful imperfections without judgment. Be fierce as you share your loving energy with the world.

Rewrite your story, but this time be victorious.

# Meditative Reflection "Word of the Day"

## MY JOURNAL ENTRY

### October 15, 2022

### Word of the Day "Oneness"

Breathe in. Breathe out.

Today, during my meditation, this was the last word that floated to me before the timer sounded for me to complete my meditation. Oneness.

There is an acceptance in my life once there is an oneness with my past decisions, celebrations, mistakes, afflictions, and misunderstandings. It cannot be changed.

When I experience oneness from a space of surrender, I no longer spend time, energy, and resources manipulating my mind to think of "if" scenarios.

The experience can't be undone. Oneness allows me to see it and make a decision to move forward. Acknowledgments don't require attachment.

Accepting something happened doesn't mean I celebrate it; it simply means it is.

Oneness is my peace. Peace can come in every experience. Peace is a decision. Peaceful thoughts connect with oneness. Oneness is a soft silence.

Oneness is an inner connection. Oneness is thankfulness. Oneness flows in my boundaries. Oneness is my comfort in the midst of a storm.

Oneness is my path to love, prosperity, abundance, and ecstasy.

## Deeper Connection Within

1. What is your story? How can you shift your thoughts from being a victim to victorious?

_____

_____

_____

_____

_____

2. How can it empower you in the future?

_____

_____

_____

_____

_____

3. How can you use it to empower others?

_____

_____

_____

_____

_____

## Gratitude Reflection of the Day

Today, I send kind and thankful thoughts to myself, honoring the growth and progress I've made on my self-love journey.

**Forgiveness Exercise of the Day:**

It's <u>One Year</u> from now.

Write a letter to yourself about the mental and emotional freedom after you choose to rewrite your memories from victim to victorious.

_____
_____
_____
_____
_____
_____
_____
_____

_____
_____
_____
_____
_____
_____
_____
_____
_____
_____
_____
_____
_____

# Set Boundaries

## Forgiveness Thought of the Day

Setting boundaries is a profound act of self-love and self-respect. It's a declaration that I value myself enough to put my well-being first. For a long time, I found myself constantly seeking permission to be happy, as if my own happiness required the approval of others. It was a tiring and unfulfilling way to live.

However, as I embarked on my journey of self-forgiveness and self-discovery, I realized that I had to shift my responses, thoughts, and behaviors to align with the boundaries I needed to create peace of mind. It meant being transparent about who I truly am, what I want, and how I deserve to be treated.

Many of my past decisions were driven by a desire to make everyone else comfortable or to gain their approval, even if it meant compromising my own needs and desires. However, I came to understand that to lead a truly blissful life, I had to start by knowing and honoring myself.

Setting boundaries became a way of showing respect not just to others but primarily to myself. It allowed me to prioritize my well-being, happiness, and inner peace. Today, I no longer wait for permission to be happy; I grant it to myself, which has made all the difference in creating a life filled with contentment and fulfillment.

**Meditative Reflection "Word of the Day"**

**MY JOURNAL ENTRY**

**September 5, 2022**

**Words of the Day "I Trust Myself"**

Breathe in and out.

Today's meditation mantra was "I trust myself."

While meditating, I drifted to what I was taught about trust as a child.

On this day, I was vulnerable and wrote my experiences with the closest people in my childhood to explore how I lost confidence in trusting myself.

What I uncovered was so intimate I decided not to share it publicly. It revealed several traumatic secret compartments that were tucked away.

This is my journal entry for that day:

After unlocking this emotional chamber and re-reading my journal entry.

I wrote the following:

I trust myself as a woman, wife, and mother.

This newfound insight into my trust in money and people just unlocked the next level of my life. I've opened the door and freed myself.

I'm so thankful.

Starting today, I define trust in my life as...

Trust is internal first.

Trust is inner facing.

Trust is defined within.

Trusting my actions.

Trusting my words.

Trusting my abilities.

Trusting my intuition.

Trusting myself.

Trusting my heart.

Trusting from my soul.

Trust starts within me and then pours out to others.

Trust others while offering space for their personal development.

When I trust myself, it opens doors to building trust with others.

I see, feel, and experience trust all around me. I trust myself with money. I trust myself in friendships. I trust myself as a wife. I trust myself as a mother. I trust my intuition.

I trust the process. I trust the journey. I trust my boundaries. I trust love.

I trust and accept God's love.

I trust.

## Deeper Connection Within

1. What boundaries do I need to create? _____

_____

_____

_____

_____

2. What would change in my life once I enforce the boundaries?

_____

_____

_____

_____

_____

3. What will happen if I do not set boundaries?

_____

_____

_____

_____

## Gratitude Reflection of the Day

I'm grateful for the courage it takes to build confidence in myself, knowing that it is a gift I give to myself.

## Forgiveness Exercise of the Day:

Write a letter to yourself about what trust means to you.

_____

_____

_____

_____

_____

_____

_____

_____

_____

_____

_____

_____

_____

_____

_____

_____

_____

_____

_____

_____

_____

_____

_____

*DAY 21*

# BE CLEAR ON YOUR INTENTIONS

**Forgiveness Thought of the Day**

Forgiving myself first has been a transformative journey, one that I've come to embrace as a continuous process rather than a final destination. I've learned I'll never have all the answers, but that's okay. What truly matters is understanding myself better and embracing my authentic self, imperfections, and all.

In this ongoing journey, I've found it crucial to clarify my intentions for various aspects of my life: wealth, finances, spirituality, physical well-being, emotional state, and mindset growth. By setting clear intentions, I've been able to define my path and shape my destiny.

It's easy to be influenced by the opinions and expectations of others, but I've learned to tune out the noise and focus on what truly matters to me. My journey of self-forgiveness has allowed me to prioritize my well-being and happiness, making my intentions all the more meaningful and aligned with my authentic self.

As I navigate life, I recognize that the journey is a beautiful unfolding, a continuous exploration of who I am and what I want to become. It's a journey filled with self-discovery, self-love, and the constant pursuit of growth and authenticity. And with each step I take, I clarify my intentions and move closer to the life I desire and deserve.

**Meditative Reflection "Word of the Day"**

**MY JOURNAL ENTRY**

**October 15, 2022**

**Words of the Day: "All of Me"**

Beautiful Obsession with *All of Me*.

Whispering, "I love you" as I sit alone in a room.

During this time of isolation for escalation, I woke up making poems for myself.

*Mirror, mirror on the wall. I love myself most of all.*

*Mirror, mirror on the wall. God's grace protects me from it all.*

*Mirror mirror on the wall. I love my reflection most of all.*

Something has shifted as I built my self-love. I accept myself and honor my love as more than enough to heal me. I cherish the light I share with the world but always use it to light my path forward.

The depth of love. The value of love. Nurturing love. Self-love. Inner love. Peaceful love.

Connected love. Delightful love. Healing love. Forgiving love. Happy love. Graceful love.

Tender love. Unconditional love. Accepting love. Receiving love. Giving love. Moving forward in love. Letting go of unhealthy attachment. Compassionate love.

Reflective love. Whole love. Sustainable love. Pieces of love. Enlightened love.

Harmonious love. Reconnected love. Profound love. Passionate love. Grace-filled love.

Inclusive love. Reunited love.

I ask for love.

I receive love.

I welcome love.

I believe in love.

I am love.

## Deeper Connection Within

I am forgiving because I want _____
_____.

I am forgiving because I need _____
_____.

I am forgiving because I deserve _____
_____.

I am forgiving because I feel _____
_____.

I am forgiving because I see _____
_____.

I am forgiving because I love the feeling of _____
_____.

I am forgiving because _____
_____.

I am forgiving because I am _____
_____.

I am forgiving because I can _____
_____.

I am forgiving because I choose _____
_____.

**Gratitude Reflection of the Day**

Today, I am filled with gratitude for the love and appreciation I have for myself, which serves as a foundation for all my relationships and endeavors.

# P.S.

In the depths of your soul, where shadows reside,

A journey unfolds, where hearts coincide.

P.S., you whisper, as you start this new quest,

To forgive your own soul, and at last find your rest.

For forgiveness begins not in others' embrace,

But inside your own heart, in a sacred space.

P.S., let it flow, like a river unbound,

Through the scars and the wounds,
where healing is found.

In the tapestry woven of moments gone by,

P.S., be the thread of a new, brighter sky.

Let go of self-blame, let go of the weight,

As forgiveness unfolds, it's never too late.

P.S., for the choices that haunt you at night,

For the battles you've fought, and
the times you were right,

For the tears that you shed and
the joy that you've known,

Forgive yourself first, let self-love be sown.

In the mirror of grace, see your worth shining bright,

P.S., be the star in your own healing light.

For the past is a story, not your final decree,

P.S., forgive yourself, and set your heart free.

In this journey of self, let compassion take flight,

P.S., embrace forgiveness, let it be your guiding light.

For in forgiving yourself, you'll discover the key,

To a life filled with love, and the joy of just being.

Congratulations to all the readers who have completed their 21-day journaling journey, emerging on the other side empowered, confident, and ready to welcome the gift of self-forgiveness into their daily lives. You've embarked on a remarkable journey of self-discovery, healing, and personal growth, and your commitment to this process is commendable.

As you turn the page to the next chapter in your lives, remember that the power of self-forgiveness is now a part of your daily habit. Embrace this gift with open arms, for it will continue to guide and nurture you on your path to self-compassion and inner peace.

With newfound confidence, you can face life's challenges with resilience and grace. The self-empowerment you've cultivated during this journey is a source of strength that will serve you well in all aspects of your life.

As you move forward, keep your journaling practice alive. It has been a faithful companion on your journey thus far and will continue to be a source of reflection, growth, and self-expression. Use it to record your triumphs, aspirations, and ongoing self-forgiveness journey.

With your hearts open to forgiveness, may your days be filled with lightness, joy, and a deep self-acceptance. You've taken a significant step towards living a more fulfilling and harmonious life, and the possibilities ahead are boundless.

Embrace this new chapter in your life with gratitude, knowing that you've laid a strong foundation for a future filled with self-love, forgiveness, and the unwavering belief in your own worthiness. Your journey is a testament to the incredible power of transformation, and your story inspires others who seek healing and empowerment.

# Below Is A List Of All 35 Forgiveness Journals

## Written By: Tuniscia Okeke

**Available on Amazon and other major bookstores or www.forgivenesslifestyle.com**
**Instagram: @forgivenesslifestyle**
**For bulk orders: info@forgivenesslifestyle.com**

### Forgiving Yourself

Forgiving Your Body Journal

Accepting the Gift of Forgiveness Journal

Forgiving People Who Reject You Journal

P.S. Forgive Yourself First Journal

Who Do You Struggle To Forgive Journal

Forgiving Your Struggle With Addiction Journal

### Forgiving Your Parents

Forgiving Your Mother Journal

Forgiving Your Father Journal

Forgiving Your Parents Journal

### Parenthood

Forgiving and Overcoming Mom Guilt Journal

Forgiveness Journal for Fathers

Parents Forgiving Tweens/Teen Journal

Parents Forgiving Adult Children Journal

### Family

Forgiving Dead Loved One's Journal

Forgiving Family Secrets Journal

Forgiving The Bullies In Your Family Journal

Forgiving Your Siblings Journal

## Marriage

Forgiving Your Wife Journal
Forgiving Your Husband Journal
Forgiving Your Mother-
In-Law Journal

## Romantic Relationships

Forgiving Your Ex Journal
Forgiving The "New"
Woman Journal

## Teens & Millennials

Forgiveness Journals for Teens
Forgiveness Journal
for Millennials

## Religion

Forgiving God Journal
Forgiving Church People Journal

## Blended Family

Forgiving A Co-Parent Journal
Forgiveness Journal
for Stepmothers
Forgiving Your
Stepmother Journal
Forgiving Your Stepkids
Mom Journal

## Relationships

Forgiving Your Abuser Journal
Forgiving Friends Journal

## Business/Finances

Forgiveness In Business Journal
Forgiving People At
Work Journal
Forgiving Past Money
Mistakes Journal

Sending you loving energy as you
forgive, heal, and grow.
**www.forgivenesslifestyle.com**

# Thank You

Gratitude is the thread that weaves connections, and at this moment, I extend my deepest appreciation to those whose unwavering support and love have been the foundation of this 35-journal writing journey and beyond.

To my beloved husband, your unwavering confidence and support during our marriage and this writing project have been my anchor. Thank you for your belief in me. It has been a constant source of inspiration. Your love and presence in my life make my soul smile.

To my mother, your honesty and vulnerability have led to this beautiful healing journey. Your transparency has supported my healing and given me the strength to support others on their transformational journey. I will forever be grateful for your courage to tell the truth.

My dear daughter, Shantia Dajah, your reminder to give myself grace has been a guiding light. Your wisdom transcends your years. You make my heart smile.

To my incredible son, Damien, your encouragement and motivation have fueled my determination to embark on this transformative journey. Your presence in my life is a source of boundless joy.

To Ike, my dynamic youngest son, your cheering from the sidelines has been a source of motivation and warmth. Your enthusiasm lights up my days.

My sister, Tanniedra, your unwavering belief in me and our brainstorming sessions have been invaluable. You are truly a gift.

Little sister, Jazmin, your willingness to share your experiences and vulnerability has touched my heart deeply. Your courage is inspiring.

To my "business bestie," Martha Banks Hall, the Creator of Vision Words, your prayers, encouraging texts, and our deep explorations of thoughts have been a source of clarity and growth to help me birth this project.

Denise, my beautiful friend, "The Fertility Godmother," your enthusiastic voice memos have made me feel like a rock star. Your presence has been a pillar of my strength.

To Thuy, I'm deeply grateful for your accountability and sisterhood, and I hold you as the beautiful gift you are close to my heart.

To Georgette and Cristal, your cheers have lifted my spirits. Your presence in my life is a blessing.

You all hold a special place in my heart, and I thank you from the depths of my soul for being a part of my journey.